THE VASSAR OF HENRY NOBLE MacCRACKEN'S TERM, 1915-1946

E. L. Wolven, Poughkeepsie, N. Y.

MacCracken at bat

Vassar College

Vassar girls as farmerettes—1918

E. L. Wolven, Poughkeepsie, N. Y.

Daisy Chain—1915

The President as Prom man

THE
HICKORY LIMB

photo. by E. H. Haight.

PREXINKA AND PREXY STROLL ON VASSAR CAMPUS.

Then spring and summer child and wanton are,
And autumn my true love returned from far.

C. C. Wilson, '17.

THE
HICKORY LIMB

By

Henry Noble MacCracken

CHARLES SCRIBNER'S SONS, NEW YORK

1950

To
ELIZABETH HAZELTON HAIGHT
Historian of Vassar

patriae quis exsul
se quoque fugit?

CONTENTS

THE
HICKORY LIMB

ONE CLEAR CALL

THE REVEREND BROCKHURST MORGAN once wrote in an article published in *Harper's Magazine*: "That the influence of men among women—the right kind of men—is superior to that of the average woman, is one of those facts which grow upon the mind by the simple process of experience."

Not long after this general law had thus been oracled, in 1913, I too was considering the matter. As a Yale professor—assistant professor, to be exact—it was my duty to believe that however important a man might be among women, such a value was incommensurable with the desirability of continuing to teach at Yale, Mother of MEN. "You are throwing your life away to go off and teach girls at Smith College," said a frank colleague. "Leave women to women; a man's business is with men. Look at Woodrow Wilson, who hated Bryn Mawr so cordially, as he said. You'll be a fish out of water, up there."

New Haven, certainly, was a man's town. The athletes were its heroes. Men never talked to women on social occasions. They got off by themselves for real talk. But perhaps Yale went a bit too far in accentuating the masculine. There were other points of view.

There were men in some cities who designed women's dress, coiffure, and complexion. Men artists painted portraits of women without loss of caste. Physicians healed women, and specialized in the art. Might not a man design a pattern of education for women, if a design were needed, and still respect himself as man? I knew, of course, how men in western universities la-

1

mented their "sissy" courses, as they dubbed the arts. But was this reasonable?

Was teaching always to be celibate and monastic? I was deeply interested at the time in the women's movement for economic equality and for suffrage. With my wife, Marjorie Dodd MacCracken, I had stood in Hyde Park, London, for an entire afternoon, watching Mrs. Pankhurst and her inspired daughter Christabel, as they fought for a hearing. An instinct for fair play drove me to listen to them. Their eloquence won my assent. From that day I was for women's votes. I attended meetings to plan the local campaign then shaping up in New England. I heard the Vassar leader, Inez Milholland, more beautiful but less appealing than Christabel. The image of the English girl, as she tried to make herself heard above the roar of the London mob, was still with me. I could hear their song:

> Put me among the girls,
> Them with the golden curls,
> Please do me a favour,
> And put me among the girls!

When things got that far, victory was near. The reaction of reason would soon come. A few men on their side might help. Later, when I spoke on platforms with Carrie Chapman Catt and Anna Howard Shaw, I would think back to these days of consideration.

I had worked on civic committees in New Haven, and had helped to make a survey of its dives and dance-halls. We had come forward with a proposal of policewomen as one means of checking the worst features of the matter. A howl of derision went up from the respectable folks. I was told to let it alone. I joined the Connecticut Society for Social Hygiene, to work through more organization and better techniques in the field.

But I was teacher of the English language. I was not disposed to devote myself to the cause of women as a career, or to the art of pleasing women, or even of influencing women, delightful as any one of these prospects might be. After all, a mind was a mind, whether it was a man's or a woman's. As a profession, I theorized, teaching took no account of sex. I should take a job at a women's college as readily as at a men's college, but no more readily. I had already had some experience in teaching women, at Simmons College, to earn money for my graduate studies at Harvard. My pupils were teachers in Boston public schools. They came tired at night to the class. Once a woman raised her hand to ask a question. I turned from Keats to her. "Are those wild geese I hear outside?" she said. I listened. It was the honk of an auto to its mate, upon the Fenway. I knew where the tame goose was, anyhow.

At Yale I was teaching women as part of my job. The university was offering extension courses to teachers at Bridgeport and New Britain, trying to stave off a movement for a state university by going out to the people. My students were older and more serious than my undergraduates in Sheffield Scientific School, and they were working for credits which when properly packaged would mean better salaries for them. But all that did not explain the difference in attitude between the two groups. More of them seemed genuinely to enjoy their own minds, to be infected with the fever of intellectual curiosity, to seek the connection between art and life.

My students at Yale, on the other hand, divided themselves into two kinds pretty sharply: those who were sent to college by parents who wanted their sons to grow up in a place which was safe and which would insure good business connections later; and those who were bent on making their own way to success and fortune. The "sent" group made the best of their lot by a merry life and often a short one. The "went" group kept their eyes fixed on the main chance. Neither had much time to waste on literature, or the use of the mother-tongue. There were of course exceptions.

The Sheffield term was three years. For students who

avoided Latin by electing the "select" course, this seemed long enough for the mere growing up. For the hard-worked students in engineering, it meant a desperately crowded week, with adequate time for no subject. My own work was thus split between hurried conferences with men too tired to listen and lazy classes whose interest I tried desperately to arouse.

Social ties with Yale and New Haven were very pleasant. They were not strong enough, however, to stand any real strain. Such came in 1913, when our oldest child, "Wee" Noble, died from a sudden attack of erysipelas. He seemed to us a very precocious boy, with unusual gifts of endearment, and we were hard hit. In that summer I lost my brother George. We had been the closest friends. Some compelling interest was needed to carry me over these great empty spaces, for somehow I seemed to lack the power to pull myself along.

The offer from Smith looked like a lifesaver, and I grasped it. The Director of Sheffield let me off with a semester's notice, and I began my work at once in the new post, but teaching at both colleges. This meant a plunge into a full schedule totalling twenty-six hours of lectures, and many more of conference, at least three times the amount now commonly expected. There was a four-hour train ride every day in the bargain, which gave time for reading the scores of themes that flooded my desk. My courses at Smith in drama and literary criticism were new to me, and I managed to keep just a week ahead of my students.

Even in this program I could not help contrasting my students at the two ends of the college highway. Sometimes there was a connection. During one conference a girl suddenly began to laugh at my strictures.

"What is funny?"

"Oh, it's just how things are. My brother is in your class at Yale. He told me you would scold, but did not mean it. Go ahead, make it good."

We became friends, and I was proud of her scenario writing

a few years later. No boy at Yale would have dared his professor
to do his worst.

I found in this healthy give-and-take with my Smith students
something very different from the docility that had driven Woodrow Wilson to madness at Bryn Mawr. He had complained that
his students put down his merest jokes in their notebooks. It
was not like that at all. "You weren't very gisty today, professor," one of them said. "Four pages, and I usually make six."

"Gisty," I found, meant "solid for notes." I hated lectures,
but with enormous classes there was no escape. So I slaved away,
trying to bring up my talks to this exacting standard. I found
a similar trait at Vassar, when more than one class complained
that men professors, especially new men, set their assignments
too low. "We took this course in good faith, and we want to be
taken seriously. We are not children."

But docility has a truer and older meaning than that which
Wilson used. It fitted these young women well. They were really
docile, apt for teaching, in the best sense. It took no effort to
win their assent to the process, such as I had found at Yale.
There the boys settled back on their haunches, with an air of
"educate me if you can." I could buck it, but the effort to get
back of this crust of indifference was tedious.

So I saw no more of the agreeable Graduates' Club at New
Haven, where I had spent many a pleasant time listening to
Uncle Toby, as my chief Wilbur Cross was known to us all, and
to Thomas Lounsbury, his famous predecessor. They loved good
crackerbarrel talk about the ills of the age. Lounsbury sympathized with my feelings on what he called the "infinite capacity
of the undergraduate mind to resist the intrusion of knowledge."
His was the famous "a few more pearls, gentlemen," when the
bell sounded and the classes scraped their feet.

The gay Lawn Club crowd had pressed Marjorie and me into
service as "perpetual chaperones" because our interest in each
other made us helpfully negligent in that fast fading task. We

had danced and housepartied till all hours; but we said goodby for good.

In other ways than students' attitudes, I found comparisons not unflattering to Smith College. It was a large and liberal place. The little New England town sheltered George W. Cable and Gerald Stanley Lee, and had traditions of its own. Smith was rapidly growing, and was easily the largest of the women's colleges. At its head was a man who really loved his job, and was in the high tide of his success.

Marion Burton was a new type to me. Basically, he was the clergyman-president of American tradition. He had come to Smith College from Plymouth Church in Brooklyn, and his pulpit style was modelled on Henry Ward Beecher. Outwardly, he was the extrovert incarnate. Inside his magnificent shell, he was soft and sensitive, and he leaned heavily upon his strong wife. Well built but slender, six feet two or more, with a shock of red hair and the white skin that goes with it, Burton was the idol of Smith girls. His gaiety was infectious, his smile all-conquering. They sang to him on every occasion: "We love you, there's none above you." They followed him along the walks. He revelled in it, but kept his head, for he was ambitious.

He had a plan to make Smith a great women's university, buying the whole of "Dippy Hill," the ground of the state asylum for mental patients—he would have brought it about, too, if he had stayed. But not long after I left Smith, Burton went to the University of Minnesota as its president, then to the University of Michigan. It was he who put Calvin Coolidge in nomination at the Republican convention of 1924. His sudden death a few months later was all that kept him from a senatorship and, perhaps, the presidency. In temperament, he had the buoyancy and charm of Franklin Roosevelt, the same reckless daring in projecting programs, and the same tendency to play hunches. We were congenial and warm friends from the first.

In the tradition of his day, Marion Burton was an amiable despot. Having offered me the position of professor at three thousand a year ("Can you teach drama?" "Yes." "Good.") and receiving my acceptance, he took me from his office to the parlor of Miss Mary Augusta Jordan, the redoubtable head of the department of English, and announced me as her new colleague. Professor Jordan was twice my age, and had a mind of her own. Nevertheless, such was the tyranny of the time that she meekly accepted this cuckoo in the nest.

I departed to break the news to Yale, which bore the news gracefully. Of course I could not be permitted to desert on such short notice; but Director Chittenden offered a compromise, by which I should teach full time at each college for a semester before going to Smith for good. Uncle Toby Cross was not unwilling, and arranged my schedule so that I taught on alternate days at New Haven and Northampton, and spent most of my time on the trains.

Professor Cheever of Chapin House welcomed me hospitably to the college guestroom in the dormitory over which she presided. This was my first introduction to the merry life of a women's college "dorm." High-pitched voices, usually tense with some excitement, competing for attention with other tensions, soon rise almost to the breaking point. Smith houses were under direct control of their "house mothers," and some measure of discipline resulted.

The department of English, of which Miss Cheever was a member, suffered from the usual rivalries of the system. Professor Mary Augusta Scott pitted herself against the world, a feminist of the first order, who had insisted successfully on the withdrawal of a book on the Italian Renaissance which, she alleged, had used her own doctoral studies unfairly. I became her good friend, for she was a real scholar, and was in a difficult position in the department. She left her estate of over $20,000 to Vassar, her college.

Since both Miss Scott and Miss Jordan were Mary Augusta, the talk at department meetings consisted chiefly of:

"Mary Augusta, you are mistaken."

"Mary Augusta, you will not listen to reason."

"Now, Mary Augusta—"

"Now, Mary Augusta—"

The rest sat around embarrassed, while their elders quarrelled.

A pleasant companion was the only other man, "Bunny" Abbott, son of the famous Lyman Abbott, editor of the *Outlook*. He had been at Smith a number of years, and was resigned to a quiet corner.

Miss Jordan, also a Vassar woman, was a real personality. Small and wiry, she was portentous in her wrath and cryptic with inspiration. A great talker, she often found her words running far ahead of her ideas, and ending in complete incoherence. It was an entertaining exercise to try to detect the exact point at which sound took command over sense. She was sharp, devastating, and even cruel at times; at other times she was kindness itself. She hated cant, banality, and all mechanical forms of speech; life with her must be always tense and at strife with something.

Miss Jordan had a famous course in John Dryden, of all poets. The old turncoat was used as a penmanship model for the hundred and fifty students, Miss Jordan's personality supplying the rest. Except for Harvard's Copeland, I had never seen such theatrics in the classroom. As a course in Mary Jordan, the class was an unqualified success, and the subject was not unworthy of understanding. Miss Jordan was an epitome of her time and group.

We got along famously. At heart, she was a motherly person, and the young professor and his wife became her children. She gave us the story of Smith, a college run by men for women. She knew Marion Burton to the innermost source of his big, flamboyant self, a somewhat hollow shell, but made up of all the ingredients of the American success story. She told me many tales of Clark Seelye, first president, who still lived up on the Hill above the college, with his iron will and terrific blasting wrath, a minor prophet of old New England. He ran the college from his wife's rocking-chair, which he had appropriated. The little sewing-drawer under its arms served him for all he needed of memoranda of appointments. One day a teacher disappeared; she simply was not. No one knew what had happened, until Miss Mary, bolder than the rest, ventured to ask Dr. Seelye what had become of the lost colleague. "She scolded me," was Seelye's only answer.

On Thanksgiving Day we had a taste of the old fellow. He read the One Hundred and Thirty-sixth Psalm, every verse of which ends with the great refrain; "For his mercy endureth forever." It was a magnificent performance, Dr. Seelye's chanted antiphon ringing out with ever increasing vigor, until it rose to a shout of triumph. There was more righteousness than mercy in the refrain, it seemed to me. But it left no doubt that Seelye was one of the great personalities of his time. I have heard nothing like it at Harvard or Yale. I sought his friendship, and valued it.

One day in the spring of 1914, as I was collecting my themes in the English office, Miss Jordan said to me: "You know that Vassar is looking for a president. Have you any suggestion for them?"

"Brother John," I said. "He would be perfect."

"Write to my brother-in-law, George Dimock, about him," she said. "He is chairman of the executive committee."

So I did. I went home, and composed a rather long letter, outlining first the kind of president a women's college ought to have, pointing out the great opportunity such a post held at the time, and arguing for my brother's complete fitness for the job. No reply came for a long time. When it came, it was purely formal.

Marjorie, with little Maisry, was living at Amherst. Finding no house for rent in Northampton, and liking Smith in every way, we had determined to build our dream house, for which we had planned ever since our marriage. Whenever we went on a train, pencil and paper came out and we planned our house.

In seven years we had worked it out. We found seven acres over in the unfashionable part of town, across the brook. A grove of beech trees covered the flat crest, on the edge of Northampton meadows, looking south away to Mt. Tom and Mt. Holyoke, and the Oxbow, a bayou of the Connecticut River. In spring the river rose in flood over the meadows, and the flotsam wood was gathered in to serve our fireplaces.

Upon the beech-bark every pair of lovers for a hundred years had carved their initials, and "The Tryst" was the inevitable name. Richard Henry Dana III, a charming young architect, drew our plans, and a good contractor, who lived in one side of a two-family house occupied in the other side by Mayor Calvin Coolidge, built it well. In later years the ex-president bought the house, calling it The Beeches; and it was there he died.

My cousin, Mrs. Dwight Hills of Amherst, lived in an old house next to Martha Dickinson Bianchi, editor of her Aunt Emily's poems. On the other side another Hills house stood vacant, and this we rented during building time. I motored daily over to Smith. In the summer days, President Meiklejohn and I played tennis daily on the Amherst courts. We were evenly matched, though the president always seemed to me to play in a perversely logical way. I came to like him as a companion, but his quick sparkling talk was beyond my skill to match.

I was working away on a book of twenty plays of Shakespeare, having just finished a college text of Chaucer in 1913. Tucker Brooke and John Cunliffe were my fellow-editors. It was a labor of love, and I came to know the famous lines by heart. The old house was surrounded by overgrown spruce planting that darkened every window. Red plush curtains still further gloomed my study, and I worked in hot sunny days by lamplight.

I was summoned one day by Marjorie to meet some visitors. I came with ill grace, for my proof sheets were upon me, and I had a deadline to meet for the coming fall. Our visitors were Charles M. Pratt and his wife Mary Morris, sister of Mrs. Hadley at Yale. They explained their call as a friendly one. Mr. Pratt asked me about my work at Smith and my current studies, rather unnecessarily, I thought. I answered briefly, and excused myself, to go back to my impatient proof sheets. I had no suspicion that Mr. Pratt was the patron and most powerful trustee of Vassar.

As the weeks passed, I grew impatient, and wrote Mr. Dimock again, urging John's case. This brought an answer. John and I were asked to meet Mr. Pratt and Mr. Dimock at the home of Mr. and Mrs. Henry M. Folger, at Glen Cove. Mrs. Folger was the third of the Jordan sisters, her husband a Standard Oil president, and at the time collector of the great Shakespeare library now in Washington.

So to Glen Cove John and I set out, he most unwillingly, and mostly to please me. He was at the time a sort of vice-chancellor of New York University. Our father had called him back to help him after an attack of illness that left the aging Chancellor worn out. So until 1910 John had really managed the University, with the title of Syndic. In 1910 when Father retired and Chancellor Elmer E. Brown succeeded him, John had stayed on, though not too happily. Father had wanted his son to succeed him, and John had had too much authority to return with good will to a subordinate post.

We lunched at the Folgers in a merry party, and John had then an hour with Mr. Pratt. I talked with Mr. Dimock and Mr. Folger meanwhile. Then we returned by the ferry to Mamaroneck, where John lived with Edith on Orienta Point.

John said to me: "They want you, not me."

"Nonsense!" I said. John said nothing, as was his custom.

A few days later a letter came from Mr. Pratt, thanking us for presenting John's case, and saying that the trustees had decided not to consider it further. I was indignant. Obviously the trustees did not know a good man when they saw one. But I could not deny they had been fair enough, and so in dudgeon I dropped the whole thing. Meanwhile Lafayette College began to make overtures to John, and whatever disappointment he had soon faded.

Our baby Joy had come in May, and Marjorie was busy. She was this kind of woman: that I slept through the whole night when the baby came, although I was in an adjoining room. The baby came before the doctor; luckily Miss Hood was an extraordinary nurse, and all went well. Our aunt, Miss Sara Dodd (Aunt Sis), was in great wrath next morning, for she, too, had been left to sleep through the whole night.

October came, and Smith absorbed my days; I thought no more of Vassar. Miss Jordan looked speculatively at me once or twice, but said nothing. The house went on to completion with deliberation. We rented rooms near the college and waited impatiently. One night the adjacent house, a three-story wood apartment, burned to the ground. Burton came down, and we worked together with volunteer firemen to get the occupants safely out. Luckily, there were back porches, which we reached with ladders. Some of the faculty were more worried about their public exposure in nightgowns than about the danger to their lives. However, we had no loss of life, though one old lady landed with her nightgown over her head.

Smith seemed an ideal place for our long pull. My classes were lively and responsive. I had my work in hand. The library was adequate. Classroom periods were banked: 9, 10, and 11 o'clock, Mondays, Tuesdays, Wednesdays. The rest of the week was one's own. In practice, the conferences were held in the first half of the week. With this schedule the Avon Swan was put to bed in short order. I signed a contract for a manual of good English with Macmillan.

Under Marion Burton's benevolent tyranny, there was little work for the faculty as a parliamentary body. At the first meeting of the year Professor Stoddard played a mild joke on his colleagues. He proposed that the faculty, not having any important legislative program, restrict its meetings to the afternoon of the fourth Wednesday of each month. The faculty solemnly acceded, and they went home and consulted their calendars. They found the following schedule:

4th Wed. of	Oct.	Mountain Day, a holiday.
"	"	" Nov.	afternoon a holiday, Thanksgiving.
"	"	" Dec.	Christmas vacation.
"	"	" Jan.	between 1st and 2nd semesters, a holiday.
"	"	" Feb.	Washington's Birthday, holiday.
"	"	" Mar.	Spring vacation.

Thus by their own vote there would be no meeting till the last Wednesday of April. Those were the days.

I was of Dr. Stoddard's mind. In coming to Smith I had made it a condition of the acceptance that I should be put on no faculty committees, and that time outside of classroom should be wholly my own. Burton applauded the move, and granted it. In my view, as in Stoddard's, nine-tenths of committee time spent by teachers in the offices of dean and registrar were wasted. Like the investigating committees of Congress, their reason for being was mostly jealousy and suspicion of executive officers.

Stoddard, by the way, a delightful companion, was busily engaged upon the physics of a billiard ball, and was planning similar attacks upon a baseball.

The house went merrily on to completion. We found in the sea sand of the cellar a tusk of a narwhal, at a depth of six feet. Mr. Canning, the college superintendent, laid out a lovely garden and a tennis court. Winding paths led down to the meadows, where we set a wading pool for little Maisry, fed by a tiny spring. With shingled walls the color of beech bark, and roof and window blinds the color of beech leaves, the camouflage was startling. The new house looked as if it had been in place through the whole century that our ancient property deed witnessed.

Then the blow fell. A letter from Uncle Toby Cross was my first intimation that the Vassar case was still open. Professor McIlwain invited us to meet Miss Florence Cushing, "of the Vassar Trustees," at dinner. We found her charming, slender and bony as a shad, but tough as drawn steel wire. Next came a dinner in Brooklyn at Mr. Pratt's home, attended by the whole Vassar committee. There were several ministers among them, Dr. Sanders and Dr. Rhoades being chief, who kept the table in a roar with a ceaseless flow of anecdotage. In the social code of the time no reference was made either to Vassar or to education in general. I was disappointed beyond measure, for I had come prepared to defend the view that the students were the college, and the rest of us, trustees, teachers, and staff, were their servants, not parental substitutes.

But not a word was said that gave me an opening. I was effectually bottled up, and remained a mere manikin. My table manners, and drinking of a demi-tasse, were covertly inspected.

Not long after, Mr. Pratt himself made the trip to Northampton, and sent for me to call upon him in his bedroom at the Plymouth Inn. It was a most painful experience. He had wrought himself to a high tension of nerves, and felt that the occasion demanded something of the sublime, which, however, he was unable to supply. Nothing of importance was said, beyond the bare fact of my election to the presidency of Vassar, and yet the whole meeting was heavy with doom and gloom. I accepted with solemnity and a terrible pain in the head. We agreed on a date of announcement, and I rushed back to Marjorie.

"What happened? Is it all right? What did he say?"

I rushed to a couch and flung myself down.

"Get me a cold wet towel. My head is splitting."

"But what did he say? What happened?"

"I've accepted. The towel!" I groaned, and turned my miserable face to the wall.

"How much is the salary?" asked practical Marjorie.

"Good Lord, I never asked, and he never told me."

So when the headache had gone, and my own tense nerves relaxed, I wrote a letter of acceptance and timidly asked what my pay should be. Our letters were written in longhand, on very small social stationery, such as ladies used at the time. In due course a tiny note came back, asking if six thousand dollars would be fair. It would.

Then on a December day after Thanksgiving, came the announcement. The New York papers carried on one day the announcement of John's acceptance of the presidency of Lafayette, on the next my own appointment. The news flash started a little interest, even though the European war was in its first half year.

I recall the quiet afternoon at Father's tea-table in Octan, at University Heights, when John and I told the ex-Chancellor of our succession to the gold stripe on his gown. He had not heard a word about it. It seemed somehow to certify his life as soundly planned.

Mother came into the room. "Noble," she said, as she had said a thousand times before, "do sit up straight. Look at your father. If you don't sit like him, you will never be a college president." A shout of laughter bewildered her, and she took the news in tears and laughter, while I played ramrod.

The day at Smith, planned by Burton, was a good show. In John M. Greene Hall, the redheaded young president made a superb speech of announcement and introduced me.

I could not measure up to his eloquence, nor was there any need. I said:

"None of this is really true, you know. We are just a part of the Red King's dream. What if he should wake up?"

There was a gasp of dismay at my lèse-majesté in calling their idol the "Red King," and then the reaction came. Innumerable Smith women have recalled the incident to my mind in the years since.

Meanwhile Mr. Charles M. Pratt summoned separately the faculty and students of Vassar to hear the glad tidings of my election. In a speech to the teachers which none of them could understand he rambled on to the mystified group, coming out at last with the name. They were dumbfounded. Not one had ever heard of me. Why should they? I had written an obscure thesis on an unknown poet of the fifteenth century, and had taught elementary English at Yale's great spelling bee to illiterate Sheffnecks—Yale's nickname for the roughneck engineers of Hillhouse Avenue. Nevertheless, like the good sports they were, they rallied and sent me a telegram of goodwill. At least I was a professional teacher, not a clergyman, like all Vassar's presidents hitherto. Not even a Baptist, like the Vassars, the Rockefellers, and the Pratts. Moreover, I had for a year at least chosen to teach women. It might have been worse.

At the vesper service in Vassar Chapel, the students, perhaps ironically, sang:

> "Hark, the herald angels sing
> Glory to the new-born king."

Mr. Pratt then announced my name with merciful brevity. A shout of laughter discomfited the speaker when he told them, no doubt to win their sympathy, that I was very young, just past my thirty-fourth birthday. Very young, indeed! Thirty-four was advanced middle age, to their way of thinking. But they, too, sent me a word of welcome. Some thought he had said eighty-four.

We had moved into the Tryst, though it was still unfinished. Mercifully, too, it was minus a telephone and a doorbell, and people left us alone after finding Marjorie and me in work clothes unpacking our belongings. Vassar graduates, curious to see the outlander at Smith, began to haunt my lectures, and my liberty was much hampered thereby. A reporter asked me whether I could explain why Vassar had not chosen a woman. I answered truthfully, that I didn't know: I supposed most of them didn't want the job, and the market must be pretty low in college material.

Another piece of publicity gave me more cause for embarrassment.

Enterprising students on the board of the Vassar *Miscellany News* wrote to Smith College for some information about their new colleague. Mary Jordan responded with a blast of jubilee that must have completely flabbergasted the young editors. They rallied, however, and the encomium was actually printed in the February issue. It remains a classic of overstatement. Miss Jordan had discovered me, and she cackled in wild triumph:

"Anima ejus in bonis demorabitur," she began. "It is a good thing that Henry Noble MacCracken is young." He writes "with incisive charm and attractive brilliancy." After a brief review of Vassar's history, she wound up to a terrific climax with a stanza from Kipling: "Oh, East is East, and West is West," etc. The exact relevancy of the stanza she did not deign to explain.

She quoted President Eliot about the importance of "preserving useful families in democratic society." My religious influence would be "free from any suspicion of professionalism"—in other words, I was no clergyman. "No awkwardly sharp lines are drawn between his public and private interests, or between his work and play. In modern scientific phrase, he functions very perfectly." (This last remark brought chortlings from all my male acquaintance.)

"Personally, Dr. MacCracken has almost as many good qualities as the night has eyes. His bodily presence is that of the once typical Ohioans, whose thinned ranks General Sherman reviewed with such stern pride at the close of the Civil War," etc. Tarantara!

She concluded on a note of heroic self-denial: "For his friends and fellow members of the Smith College Faculty, the Vassar call is so clearly that of a manifest destiny, that a falter on their part would be sin." Her faith was justified. Like their fellow townsman, Calvin Coolidge, Smith professors were "against sin," and they did not falter as they heroically bade me farewell.

Christmas holidays came, and our first visit at Vassar. Marjorie had never seen it. My last visit had been twelve years before, when I had squired a friend at a college dance, and gone on a senior boatride past West Point. The corridors and stairwells of old Main Building were not then shut away for fire prevention, and were crowded with envious sophomores perched in windows and on the stairs eyeing us speculatively. We had danced twosteps and waltzes in regular alternation as prescribed on the dance-cards. Main dining-room was then one story high, and was filled with square pillars, against which we caromed off when crashed into by gallant heroes of Princeton, eager to display their powers of backing all the way down the hall without once looking behind.

The chartered steamboat next day took us in the sentimental twilight up and down the river, while we sang the repertory of Vassar songs, or were otherwise engaged. Amy Reed's "An institution once there was" and "Shlinga da ink" are the only ones I remember.

This winter day in December, 1914, offered no place for sentiment. We rode instead in very plushy Pullman. It was my first ride in a chair-car, and gave me an agreeable sense of great extravagance. Mr. and Mrs. Pratt were with us, and were very kind. In a cryptic way he alluded to little differences of opinion among the Vassar faculty and trustees. I could make nothing of it.

We started from the station at Poughkeepsie in an old rickety taxi which broke its axle while negotiating Raymond Avenue corner at high speed—fifteen miles—while we floundered down the icy road the rest of the way. As we entered the gate, a sad prophetic procession greeted us. The new art building, Taylor Hall, was almost completed, and the plaster casts which then made up most of Vassar's art collection were on their way across the campus from Avery Hall, where they had ruled since 1870. Tortured Laoköon writhed his way across the snow, the Wingless Victory staggered along behind him, and Father Tiber took life easy on the skids. It seemed symbolic of something.

Soon we met the faculty, such as could be summoned to

leave their town and college dwellings. They were curious but friendly. Herbert L. Mills, Professor of Economics and chairman of the faculty during the interim year, was particularly kind. He assured me that there had been no faculty candidate—usually fatal to a newcomer's success—that he himself preferred teaching, and the way was clear to cordial relations. This was good news.

That evening, however, there was a sharp tilt at a committee meeting for planning the Fiftieth Anniversary the next fall. The trustees were determined to center this upon an inauguration, the faculty equally determined to prevent it. The talk became acrimonious, and I offered to leave, but the teachers gave in at this, and surface calm returned. The antagonism was not disguised.

Meanwhile my wife explored the President's house. The style was English "detached villa," and she liked it. Miss Florence Cushing, her escort, had insisted the men trustees were neglectful of the amenities of life, and had been at once appointed Chairman of a Committee on Amenities. She had happily engaged a decorator, and planned our house as it was to be for thirty-two years. Neither of us was inclined to urge the spending of a lot of money on ourselves, and some of the wallpaper stayed with us to the last. We did ask, however, that the cracks in the brick walls be pointed up, and this was done some years later. The masons found over a hundred pounds of honey in the walls. We made bonfire of the stuff; it burned with a beautiful violet flame.

DR. TAYLOR'S COLLEGE

ON OUR WAY TO VASSAR we called on President and Mrs. Taylor, who were living at the Gotham in New York. It was not the first time I had met Vassar's "Prexy." In '98, as the guest of Jane Belcher, I had come up to a junior prom. "Come and meet Prexy," said Jane.

"No, let's dance. I don't want to waste a minute." Jane took me by the ear. She was the athletic type, as strong as any one of her four brothers who were my college mates at New York University. I twisted and writhed, but it was no use. Short of knocking her out, and it was doubtful if I could do that, I had no choice but to follow. We went down the line.

"Prexy, here's a boy that doesn't want to meet you."

Prexy Taylor burst into a high infectious splash of laughter. I've never heard anything like it, except William Howard Taft's chuckle.

"You can let go now, I've got him," said Taylor, with a crushing hand-grip. So we met.

Sixteen years had abated none of the vivacity and personal charm of this extraordinary man. In 1914 he had just ended twenty-eight years as president of Vassar, and was enjoying his freedom like a colt in a field, as he put it. He looked back on the office as a crushing burden, and wondered that he had lasted so long. Confined to his desk, his exuberant vitality had made him corpulent, but his manner was as energetic as ever.

I tried to get his counsel for my first days at Vassar, but he would not be drawn out. Finally I made one last appeal.

"Dr. Taylor, I want to take with me one word of good counsel, at least. You cannot refuse me that."

He thought a minute.

"Well, I'll tell you one thing. Don't put a telephone in your house. You'll regret it if you do."

Our call ended in gay laughter as Prexy spun his anecdotes.

James Monroe Taylor was one of the most successful leaders in a generation of famous captains of education. The period 1885–1915 was an era of confident expansion, directed by men who had been forced by the spirit of the times into the role of dictators. Woodrow Wilson, W. R. Harper of Chicago, Butler of Columbia, were the type specimens of a whole group. Most of them had encountered stormy times, but their mark upon their college's life would never be lost. In a sense that would not occur again, Taylor *was* Vassar in 1914. When he retired in February, 1914, the graduates felt lost. No one could fill his place.

Taylor had come to Vassar from successful pastorates. His wife, Kate Huntington, was like himself from the strong Baptist center, Rochester. One of her cousins, Calvin Huntington, gave an endowed scholarship to Vassar, restricted to his relatives, and requiring that if the recipient should be of collateral descent outside the male line, she must take Huntington as her middle name. The family affection and keen personal interest marked all the relations of Taylor and his college.

Like the other heads of small colleges in that day, Dr. Taylor had for years performed all the duties of president, dean, professor of philosophy, (and in his case psychology as well) public relations, admissions, records, business manager, and treasurer. He wrote all the college correspondence with his own hand. He toured the schools and recruited students, visited graduates and called on rich men to beg funds. He chased trespassing young men off the grounds. I have been told by some of them that he was as fleet-footed in those days as an Oxford "bulldog." He won his girls forever for their college.

Here's to our Vassar
There's none can surpass her.

They meant it, though the rhyme might jangle. They threw
themselves into Vassar's cause with a fervor unknown before.
For "Prexy Taylor" they gave and named a gate, a building, a
library fund, a scholarship, a professorship, and a stained-glass
window. They would have renamed the city for him if they had
had the vote. There was no resisting them. It was the first fine
flush of power, of strength in union, of thrill in achievement.
The college began to be, as Taylor called it, "no mean city."

The Gibson girls, "When Patty went to college," were found
to be two inches taller than their mothers, and of greater girth
everywhere but round the hips. They were fit mates for "Daddy
Long Legs," according to the author, Jean Webster. They were
amazingly efficient, most of them. They began to make the men
as well as the news columns. Marriage and birthrate of college
class reports began to rise after 1900, the low point of the educated women, when only half of them married, and to most
marriages but one child was born.

"Let's have a gay time,
A little play-time"

they sang to their sister classes. Their songs were all full of the
stirring new life. If a little complacency stole in, Dr. Taylor, I am
sure, forgave it.

With all this he literally was the life of the campus. His
figure skating was admired. His gay laughter pervaded the whole
college.

Serenades by thronging students and inspiring talks in response by "Prexy" from his porch were featured. At two visits,
at least, I had heard them, and witnessed the genuine display of
girlish affection.

"Vassar College is no mean college." That was his theme for

every speech. In an age of competition, Taylor was fiercely competitive. He insisted upon the priority of Vassar in the history of women's education. He wrote "Before Vassar Opened" to prove his point. I was reminded as I perused it of my father's story of the old parson who preached on Methuselah. He divided his sermon into two parts: who Methuselah was not, and who Methuselah was.

Taylor's second book "Vassar" was the second part of his sermon; Vassar first and last.

In great measure he succeeded. The graduates of Vassar came to think of themselves as "richly blessed," to quote an "Alma Mater" song of 1915. The intensity of their loyalty equalled the college spirit among the most devoted of their brothers, even though not whipped up by victories on the gridiron and diamond. It was, on the other hand, not watered down by fraternity bonds, class rivalries, or regional rivalry. It was all Vassar.

Who could resist such a man? Certainly not the girls of the '90's, the Gibson Girls of the straight front and the billowy bun. They came by hundreds, overcrowding the "dorms" every year, though Dr. Taylor built six large residence halls in rapid succession to house them. Still they came, and filled neighboring boarding schools, music-room cubicles, and cottages off campus, awaiting their turn to be "drawn on" the sacred field, as others left.

They sang, they picnicked on Sunset Hill in a thousand "bacon-bats," they went on river boat rides, climbed Mohonk Mountain, hiked with John Burroughs through the Catskill wilderness, biked all over the green hills of Dutchess County. They ate tons of Vassar fudge. They created the "sweet girl graduate," the "Patty" who went to college, the "Vassar Girls Abroad." To them Tin Pan Alley dedicated the "Vassar Girl Waltzes," still caricatured at campus parties.

The "Daisy Chain" wove its spells about the class trees and the enchanted newspapermen. Beginning in the nineties as an affectionate decor conceived by worshipping sophomores in honor of their senior sisters, the daisy parade gradually became scarcely less sacred than a wedding march. I could not believe my eyes when I first saw Vassar groundsmen rolling out the white carpet on the lawn, and the stately maidens, overpowering in their Florodora finery, stepping out for their rendezvous. It was the seriousness with which the whole ceremony was endowed that overpowered you. No picture ever caught it. It was, I fear, the source of all the beauty parades, the "Miss America" business.

It was this Vassar of the gay time, of the pretty, artful college miss, that caught the fancy of the age. Personality came before intellectuality.

It was, indeed, against M. Carey Thomas' ideal of intellectualism as the keynote of Bryn Mawr that Dr. Taylor set up his ideal of the "well-rounded" woman. Vassar graduates were to be cultured but human, not leaders but good wives and mothers, truly liberal in things intellectual but conservative in matters social. And this most of them dutifully became. But they never overtook the image which the public took to its heart, of the "sweet girl graduate."

Yet Taylor had responded to the intellectual need of his time as well as his limited means allowed. In a dozen years he had added professorships of history, economics, psychology, political science, and religion, and beginnings in sociology. For the humanities he built a beautiful library, for the sciences two new laboratories. One of the latter, Sanders Hall of Chemistry, was given by a trustee who had wanted to give a music building, but was talked out of it by Dr. Taylor. The grin on the little tailors on Taylor Hall of Art is slightly ironic, since Taylor did not favor Fine Art. Characteristically, the building, in the best college Gothic, has no studio, and its library was originally in its smallest room. A single classroom must suffice for instruction.

Taylor's greatest gift to Vassar was the group of really distinguished teachers he persuaded to come to its comfortable but sparsely furnished chairs. Lucy Salmon in history, Mills in economics, and Wylie in English, have all been celebrated in memorial volumes. They were really great teachers. Miss Salmon's students soon made their mark in historical scholarship, and especially in administration, for Miss Salmon's history was dynamic. Social workers swore by "Millsy," and Vassar graduates soon were pioneers in social work, a new profession. A whole group of young writers were trained by Miss Wylie, whose social criticism of literature was her contribution. The Vassar *Miscellany* was for years looked upon as one of the best college monthlies. Pulitzer Prizes were to follow.

These were but a few of Taylor's galaxy of good teachers. Margaret Washburn, who wrote "The Animal Mind," was unrivalled as a clear lecturer and inspiring guide in the seminar. Vassar trained more psychologists in her day than did many universities. Treadwell in zoology, Saunders in physics, and Moulton in chemistry were outstanding science teachers. And these were not all. I was amazed to find the quality of teaching at Vassar definitely better than that I had known at either Harvard or Yale. This was Taylor's work.

One of the safety valves of the time was intercollegiate debate. Subjects were carefully phrased, and debaters trained in a formal rhetoric that lasted until English teams came over and laughed it away with their easy give-and-take. But there was real political feeling under it all, and teams were sent off to other colleges by cheering classmates. At night in the "Soap Palace," (Main Lobby so-called from its soapy marble stairs) students would linger to sing and cheer the home team, and to get the flash from the wire that told of victory or defeat at Smith or Mt. Holyoke.

By 1915 the women's movement had become a real issue. Inez Milholland, '09, the statuesque Joan of the advancing young folks, was leading other Vassar women into aggressive tactics. I had met her in New Haven, and admired the skill with which she met a hostile group of university people by a purely intellectual defense of her position. When she returned to her college at its anniversary in 1915, she was clearly the idol of the undergraduates. The legend went that in her final ethics exam she wrote two complete papers: "The World as Prexy Thanks It Is," and "The World as It Is." Dr. Taylor with good sportsmanship gave her an "A."

In 1912 the alumnae elected to trusteeship Julia Lathrop, '80, the famous leader in social work, colleague of Jane Addams and Director of the Children's Bureau in the Federal Government. Miss Lathrop was eager to lead Vassar in a thorough reform of education. The trustees, however, would not consider her ideas. Her plan for a school of social work was later adopted by Smith College. Her plan for the study of the family and especially of child development was similarly shelved. In 1915 at the anniversary she gave a notable address on "The Highest Profession for Women." "Its aim," she said, "was to give the woman head of a household the status of a profession. Through it, instead of being isolated by the narrow life of home, the mother allies herself to the highest studies and makes invaluable contributions as a sheer by-product of her daily cares."

This did not make sense to Dr. Taylor, nor to the leading educational experts of the time. Dr. Abraham Flexner, for example, ridiculed the idea that anything resembling scholarship could be created out of housekeeping, marriage, and child-bearing. The whole of higher education for women was still governed by the concepts developed when men were the only students and women went with the land.

But to me Miss Lathrop and Miss Lillian Wald, who followed her, made very good sense. Miss Wald said: "Women have been experiencing the growth of a new consciousness, an integral element in the evolution of self-government, and as a result many more women than ever believe that *they* can best represent human interests in government, at least that they can best represent themselves in those measures that immediately concern them and for which tradition and experience have fitted them. . . . She is a freer being, capable of being more and of doing more."

As I sat in the audience that day, these words came to me like the sound of a trumpet. From that day dates Vassar's interest in the family and in child psychology, in marriage and all the social institutions with which euthenics has been concerned. The Vassar Summer Institute meets in part at least Julia Lathrop's plea for graduate training and research in family life. To her we owe Blodgett Hall and the Wimpfheimer Nursey School, and to her persuasion the approval of the trustees for major studies in the field. It was not for nine years, however, that this came about, and much water had gone down the millrace.

Today, when political science is second to English in the "majors" at Vassar, with child study a close third, it is hard to realize that such a revolution in the idea of culture could have come about in one generation.

When I recall my few talks with Dr. Taylor about those matters, it seems to me that he was not really opposed to the new trend, but that he dreaded its premature invasion of the college. He stood for standards, the highest that he knew. The advances made in the sciences of physiology, psychology, and anthropology were not then widely known. Home economics was thought of as an elementary technique. Political equality had not been tried on any large scale. Among Vassar women were some of its leading opponents. Economics was taught as a theoretical subject. Why, then, give up the purely intellectual disciplines that had come down to us in the great tradition of learning, for something so chaotic as suffrage, social work, and child welfare? Some day these movements would shake down into some mass of material that can be sifted, classified, and measured. All in good time.

Gradually, as those years passed, the new movements took over Prexy Taylor's college. In a word, Vassar outgrew him, as every college outgrows its leader, and he was among the first to perceive it. Not in affection or respect, but in intellectual standards, in political interest, and in social aims. With a strongly conservative board of trustees, Dr. Taylor held back the driving social interest pretty skillfully, up to the very year of his retirement. When the faculty boiled over in protest, he made a personal appeal to them to wait a bit.

A device of the president, approved by the board, gave one vote in faculty meeting to each department on all important questions. Thus the large departments of history, English, and economics, with thirty teachers, had the same vote as astronomy, philosophy, and music, with three teachers. In practice it meant that only heads of departments, older and generally more conservative than their colleagues, had the vote.

Thwarted in faculty expression, the social drive of teachers and students found other outlets. The Goodfellowship Clubhouse, built and endowed by students, represented their sympathy with the workers in kitchen and bakery, shop and farm, and their living conditions. When interest in suffrage ran high, students were not permitted to hold meetings on the campus, and so adjourned to the neighboring cemetery. There were trained many of the suffragist leaders. The national leader, Harriot Stanton Blatch, Vassar '78, whose mother's amendment on suffrage is now in our constitution, was not, I found, welcome on her own college campus. But by 1940 we had published her autobiography.

But Dr. Taylor knew how to work with women, nevertheless. The two women whom Maria Mitchell nominated as worthy of the president's office at Vassar were loyal co-workers for many years. Florence Cushing, '73, was one. Helen Hiscock, '73, who married her professor Truman Backus, and set a precedent that has often been followed, was a second. She served for twenty-three years. The third of that first group of women trustees, Mary Thaw Thompson, '77, though serving for but two years, was a most devoted friend of the college. When Frederick F. Thompson died in '99 after fifteen years' service, his widow Mary Clark Thompson accepted his place and was an active supporter until the end of Dr. Taylor's term.

The men far outnumbered the women on the Board, nevertheless, and Dr. Taylor made no effort to change the proportion of three women to thirty men which the alumnae had obtained in '86, after their success in forcing the resignation of President Caldwell. It was a great shock when in 1917 I suggested a more even balance. Throughout Taylor's term Vassar was a college for women developed by men.

One of Dr. Taylor's great supporters was John D. Rockefeller, who joined him as trustee in 1888, and remained till 1905. This was the formative period of Rockefeller philanthropy, which took organized shape about 1890. Vassar College was an experimental project in this greatest of all charitable enterprises, for Frederick T. Gates, Mr. Rockefeller's almoner and adviser on gifts, was also trustee from 1893 to 1905. Mr. Rockefeller's daughter, Bessie, was a Vassar student from 1886 to 1888 and married Charles A. Strong, whose father, Dr. Augustus H. Strong, was trustee from 1884 to 1918. Thus the ties were intimate. I found no evidence that Dr. Taylor influenced Mr. Rockefeller in the development of his organized giving. Strong and Davison Houses bear his mother's and his daughter's names, and Rockefeller Hall his own name. When I appealed to him for funds with which to furnish the attic of his hall, adding a dozen offices, he was quick to respond. In one of his early conditional gifts, he offered in 1904 to double anything the graduates might collect up to $200,000, but in spite of Dr. Taylor's hard work the sum was not raised in full. Dr. Taylor opposed the method and spoke out against it at the time. He called it "a killing policy" for the president.

Opposition to drives was not his only point of disagreement with the great philanthropist. Mr. Rockefeller once told me that Dr. Taylor very strongly objected to his deputation of giving to a great organization like the Rockefeller Foundation or the General Education Board. Giving, he maintained, must be personal, in order to be accounted for righteousness.

Before this happened, Taylor had been involved in the Rockefeller project that resulted in the University of Chicago. Dr. Augustus Strong, then chairman of Vassar's board and a leading Baptist clergyman, used to meet Mr. Rockefeller at Vassar, breakfasting with him in Main dining room on days when the Executive Committee met. Strong, whose imagination was almost unlimited, was pressing the philanthropist to found a great university in the East.

Another visitor to Vassar was William Rainey Harper, then a teacher of Hebrew at Yale, and a visiting lecturer in Bible study at Vassar, coming weekly to the college. Harper and Rockefeller became fast friends, and the project of a university in Chicago took rapid shape. At the Taylor home, finally—my informant was Mrs. Taylor—Mr. Rockefeller offered Harper the presidency of the university to be founded in Chicago. Harper turned to Taylor and said: "I'll take it, if you'll come with me." "No," said Taylor, "my place is here."

Harper accepted later, as everybody knows, and the great university was on its way. I do not know why such incidents are not as interesting as the tales of Oxford origins, of St. Frideswide and William of Wykeham. Some day they may be.

Vassar's generosity in making the University of Chicago her nurseling was to be repeated, in the 1920's, when the trustees loaned my spare evenings to Sarah Lawrence College for planning its development, and allowed four of the Vassar trustees to sit on the Sarah Lawrence Board for ten years, until the new craft had been well launched. There is precedent for such noncompetitive assistance, but it is not common in educational history. Like Taylor, I had made Mr. W. V. Lawrence's acquaintance because he had a most loyal Vassar daughter, and I thought he might help us. Like Matthew Vassar, Lawrence was led from other projects to that of a new experimental women's college, the success of which has been outstanding.

Taylor's refusal to join Harper in the Chicago project was not his only chance to leave Vassar. Brown University elected him president, and the joy of Vassar women at his refusal was unbounded. At last! Here was a man who believed a women's college really was a more rewarding place for a life work than one of the best colleges for men. Didn't this prove that Vassar was the best of all possible colleges?

Taylor spent two of his twenty-eight years as president on sabbatical leave, one whole year being spent in Rome and other travel abroad. Few presidents could leave their jobs with equal serenity. No one suggested that I was entitled to similar rewards, but I managed to squeeze out two semesters in thirty-two years. Sixty years of two men ought to have put Vassar in the fossil wing of the college museum, but somehow she has survived us. I ascribe it to the dynamic engendered by Prexy Taylor's vehement drive.

Among the most devoted of Taylor's trustees was Uncle Fred Thompson, who perpetrated the ugly *porte cochère* of Main Building. His widow's gift of the F. F. Thompson Library in 1904 scarcely atones for it. But Uncle Fred meant well. It was only natural to add a new wing to a building that had so many already. The covered doorway was certainly a great physical improvement over the icebound staircase of Old Main. The Soap Palace, with its rose-and-gray marble steps and panels, made a good rallying place for songs and cheers on festive occasions. The two-story library above was a real improvement over the outgrown rooms. But its days are numbered now and Uncle Fred will be forgiven.

He was the most popular of trustees. On every visit it is said that he ordered steak and ice cream for the students. He it was who "endowed" the asparagus, who gave holidays to Mohonk or steamer rides on the river. Dr. Taylor once remonstrated with him, pointing out the damage done to the schedule of teaching. "Dear Dr.," wrote Uncle Fred, "you teach em and I'll play em." An excellent division of labor between trustee and president.

It was Uncle Fred, native of Poughkeepsie by the way, but president of the great First National Bank of New York, who presented every girl graduate of the time with a souvenir teaspoon. As an example of the taste of the day, it is worth a description. Beginning at the top of the handle, sits a very grim

Alma Mater in the form of Athena, high helmeted; an olive branch springs out of her left ear and a palm branch out of her right ear. Just below is a most modern Rand McNally globe on its pedestal, and carelessly strewn about it are a telescope, a sextant, a surveyor's compass, and a box presumably containing other tools of the mathematician. Beneath this, in turn, is the traditional oil lamp of the student, and beneath this is a book; beneath this, believe it or not, are seven more books, standing upright but ready for use, and beneath this, as we reach the narrow part of the handle, are two oars tied together with a ribbon but all ready to row the proud possessor across the stormy waters of the Vassar Lake. In the bowl of the spoon stands a student in cap and gown, who is either eating a ham sandwich or leading a college cheer; her gestures are ambiguous. In the background, quite oblivious of her, other students are playing tennis. The long dress of the period must have made the game a most hazardous one. Trees in the background of the scene complete the picture, and are an attempt at the realism of the floral circle. Such is the Homeric catalogue of the front, but the back of the tea-spoon contains, surrounded by elaborate scroll work, the initials of the honored student, the words "Vassar College" and—"Sterling." Four of these famous relics are preserved in the library along with the "conscience spoons" engraved with the legendary word "Female."

Finally, Mr. Charles M. Pratt and his wife, Mary Morris Pratt, must be reckoned among the closest friends of President Taylor. Mrs. Pratt with her friend Mrs. William R. Thompson gave him the college Chapel, with its beautiful "Taylor window." From 1896 to the end of his term Dr. Taylor leaned heavily upon Mr. Pratt for counsel and practical aid on the Board of Trustees. Taylor Hall in 1914 came as a testimonial to this friendship. Out of this Jesse-tree of Vassar loyalty sprang a group of friends of Vassar. It forms so good an illustration of the relation between family ties and college loyalty that it might well be set forth in a genealogy.

With such strong support as this, Vassar prospered, though its endowment of a million and a half was meager when compared with men's colleges. But it enjoyed its reputation for prosperity. "They think some punkins of themselves at Vassar," Miss Jordan told me.

Dr. Taylor's insistence on the preeminence of his college was perhaps a subtle device for instilling courage and confidence, initiative and self-reliance, into the somewhat conventional and timid maids that began to come to Vassar after the first flood of feminism had abated. There is noticeable in the college songs of the time a kind of Tarantara reminiscent of the immortal constables' chorus. "Onward we march." "Here's to our Vassar, none can surpass her," "We are from Vassar," etc.

"Speak up yuh silly goop, yuh know the answer, yuh know yuh do," cried Miss Wylie, while her sharp but kind eyes flashed fire at the trembling freshman.

"You have a mind, use it," urged Miss Salmon.

Miss Washburn urged her students on to the study of original problems, and published forty of their papers under their names—and hers.

Gradually under this incessant spurring, timid, shy girls took heart, and began to assert themselves. Underlying it all was the feeling of security engendered by confidence in their college. When in later days I was elected honorary member of Vassar 1900, and was welcomed into their noisy, jolly comradeship, I began to see that Taylor's policy had paid off. The self-confidence sometimes became aggressiveness, but even so it was far better than the old shrinking pride.

The natural consequence of such a policy, and of adding strong teachers to the staff, was to bring the Vassar pot to boiling. " 'Tis in vain," said Matthew Vassar, "to educate woman's mind, and then limit the opperation." The two "pp's" seem to hint the force implied. Dr. Taylor at any rate found it strong, and the last few months of his term found him sitting on the lid, rather unhappily. Vassar women in a considerable majority had come to want three things; a reform of the course of study, in the direction of action based on application of science to the arts of living, in the speaking of foreign language, the writing of the native language, and the practice of fine arts; Vassar's leadership in the movement for women's emancipation, beginning with suffrage, and extending into every field of human activity; and finally, control of their own college by Vassar women.

These were fighting issues. People lost their tempers about them. There was heat as well as light in Vassar's culture, and one could not tell where the volcano would erupt. It was no wonder that Dr. Taylor destroyed all his correspondence before turning his office over to me, and that I had to begin from the egg to feel my way into the maze of conflicting tensions. But I was hardly prepared for what I found in the president's otherwise empty desk, on the day when I took over. In the right-hand drawer was a cardboard box, with the printed label "wax candles." When I opened it, I found a loaded revolver. This was Prexy Taylor's only bequest to his successor.

COME TAKE A CRACK
AT Mac CRACKEN

College Song

OUR LAST DAYS AT THE TRYST were of mixed feelings. My visit at Vassar had given me a glimpse of the battle lines in education. It was not easy to leave our dream house after six weeks of it had proved to us that the dream had been real. But chiefly I began to get stage-fright, as I realized the dimensions of my job.

Alumnae called on us out of curiosity, always saying as they left, "Well, I don't know. Of course you're not Prexy Taylor, but—"

Gallantly "Prexy" tried to protect me. At a serenade he warned them. "Don't criticize until he has been here thirty years. Give the young man a chance."

They sadly promised to tolerate the newcomer, and wiped their eyes. I began to feel that I had been let out of Smith on probation. The new psychology was beginning to talk about introverts and extraverts. It seemed to me that I belonged in both categories. At heart I was introvert, but compensated by an extravert drive. Shy and withdrawn when left to myself, I couldn't say "no" to anybody.

I attended, as one of fifty English Lit. specialists invited to join, the first session of the American Association of University Professors. One of the first motions adopted was to exclude college presidents from membership, even though they might be

35

teachers. I was astounded by the unanimity with which adoption came, and by the bitterness against presidents in every speech. Obviously I had ostracized myself by my own action from the company of scholars. There must be something fundamentally wrong with American education for such hatred to spread over the whole land. Was I to be the object of it? Hadley, at least, was respected at Yale, I recalled with some comfort. Faculty autonomy might work at Vassar, too.

January brought the term's end. There were nearly two hundred examinations to read and grade, and nearly as many long papers, with endless conference. Mrs. Conkling was a great help, but I had responsibility for the marks. I did not want to leave unfinished work behind me, nor to be bothered with the make-up work of failures. So, I raised all my failures to a pass grade, and pushed everyone else up at the same time. I left Smith in the odor of sanctity.

On the way to Vassar at the month's end, I stopped in New York to address the graduates at a Biltmore luncheon. Deciding that I might as well be hanged for a sheep as for a goose, I decided to declare the faith that was in me.

I was never much of a philosopher, but my experience at Harvard and Yale had taught me that education was too often regarded as the vested interest of the faculty. Of other vested interests I was to learn. The analogy usually made was that of a factory, in which teacher-workers turned out a product known as education. "We guarantee the quality of our product, or return the boy," President Lowell used to say jocosely, and rather cruelly, as I thought.

The analogy seemed false to me. Students were not pieces of wood and metal, but people. Moreover, even factorywise they and their parents paid the cost, and were entitled to know what they were getting. I resented the attacks on students and their parents that made up the greater part of academic grumbling. Still more I resented the high ratio of failures by students, when taught by people who did not know how to teach.

This was my chance, and I took it. I affirmed that students would be my first concern, not only because they were entitled to it, but because they were at once the source and goal, the alpha and omega, of the curriculum. As the source, the current interests of students should be carefully studied, and the material worked up in sciences and arts, with continuous recasting in the light of changing interests. For the so-called great tradition I cared nothing, except as it managed to hold the loyalty of students. As the goal of education, I asserted that students were ends in themselves, not children in leading-strings. Treated as immature, they would remain immature. Exploited by politicians, they became the spearhead of political thrusts. Public demand for amphitheatrical shows had made American football, not the students. Academic neglect of housing had produced fraternities, and alumni control drove social snobbery down the students' throats.

But in spite of all this, students had made known their interests. Political science in America was a response to American needs. So was American sociology. Other needs would create new disciplines.

All this was, of course, heresy. It started at the wrong end of everything. Modern education split off from the Roman Catholic Church in the period of the Renaissance, and set up humanism in place of authority; but it did not change much besides. What was really democratic about the American school was school life, which was beyond the control of vested interests. When I laid sacrilegious hands upon the Great Tradition and suggested that the curriculum should come from the students, I put myself beyond the pale.

In a speech a few weeks later, to Washington alumnae, I went further. I called it "The Fetich of the Grove," and suggested that we were mistaking the place for the process. There was no magic in the atmosphere of the academic. The college had no monopoly of learning. The whole city of Washington, for example, was a great national university. The fetich led to snobbery and the educated accent. The scientific verbiage, *"science Iroquois,"* as Fabre called it, was its product. Only when parents shared in the process of education was it effective. Responsibility for the student in life rests now as it has always done, upon the family.

I denounced the passive acceptance of learning, the packaging of knowledge, the hieratic cipher, the use of college as a rubber stamp for social purposes, academic intolerance, out-of-touchness, and the purchase of college time as a release from parental responsibility. Learning was the one thing needful, not these base uses.

This was going much too far. The worst was feared. Already Inez Milholland was in training to ride her white horse at the head of the Suffrage Parade on Fifth Avenue. Feminism was a theme in the issue of the *Miscellany* in which my speech appeared.

As the President's House was unready, I was asked to stay with Dr. and Mrs. Bancroft Hill, in their ever hospitable home on Professors' Row. My reëducation was at once undertaken by the older professors. I listened, but was not repentant. Good Dr. Hill initiated me into the mystery of chapel. I undertook it cheerfully, but was so frightened that I had to cling to the pulpit with both hands to support my trembling knees. I was reminded of the incident years later when Governor Roosevelt gave the commencement address, and held to the same pulpit, but with far different cause.

I left out two whole petitions of the Lord's Prayer, and thereafter read it from a card, never trusting my memory in such moments of tension. The students were kind to me, and I thought they even liked my nervous shyness.

As soon as I could, I excused myself from the constant attentions of the hospitable Hills, and took refuge in the Founder's Room, a guest chamber in old Main, with Mr. Vassar's old four-poster to sleep in, the highest bed I ever knew. There, outside of office hours, I read all I could about the Founder and his college, of which more anon. My meals were eaten at first at the famous Faculty Table in Main, where seats were held in seniority, and I sat humbly at the foot. Soon I found my way to students' tables, and was welcomed.

My first real friend among them was a freshman, whom I met in the newspaper room across the corridor. Lucille Phillips came from Los Angeles. Her grandfather had been a famous Forty-Niner, and her parents were leaders in the state. Lucille's love of life and all it gave made her outstanding. Student president in senior year, Vassar's first undergraduate war bride, author of many books in later years, her greatest ambition at the time was to have a Vassar daughter. For years after her graduation, I used to get postcards with "Darn it, another boy!" until four were counted. Then she adopted a daughter. But alas! by that time Lucille was a trustee of Scripps, in the good Vassar tradition of aiding other colleges for women, and daughter went to Scripps.

At last Marjorie came with Aunt Sis and the children, and we entered the home of thirty-two years. With us came Miss Nellie Fitzmaurice, our lifelong friend, whose "Irish Oven" later became a college institution, with famous brownies and birthday cakes. Came also Mary Walsh, who later returned to Northampton and married, and whose children entered Smith. The immediate family included Aunt Sara B. Dodd, sturdy Pennsylvanian of seventy-seven years, red-haired Maisry, five years old, and baby Joy, born at Amherst. Maisry promptly went out and invited every passing student to call on us, which proved embarrassing. We found others had been in the house before us. This was our introduction to a notorious student group whose one aim was to sleep every night in a different spot. They slept on the roof of Main Building, in the boiler house, the steam conduits, *and* every room in the President's House.

Charming Mrs. Taylor with her wonderful daughter Mary paid her first call upon us. Marjorie casually mentioned that we were Democrats. Mrs. Taylor flinched as if someone had struck her. I feared she was ill, and spoke in an undertone to Mary about it. She reassured me; Mrs. Taylor just could not face the dreadful truth that a Democrat was living in the President's House.

At the student reception I made my second friend, Mary Mallon, '15, who claimed me as "Cousin Henry" at once. The relationship was distant, but I cherished it, for Mary was a born scholar, and a wonderfully well-read woman. She was editor of the *Miscellany*, and wrote for the Anniversary year an excellent history of student government at Vassar. I was a welcome guest at her home in Cincinnati, where her father and mother were famous citizens. Later, with brothers and husband in the war, and mother overseas in the Y, Mary worked for me in '17–'18 in the Junior Red Cross in Washington.

It was mere accident, no doubt, that gave me access to the friendship of these two brilliant young women, and fixed once and for all my concept of the Vassar model. Below such a standard I was never willing she should fall.

Professor Jacques Barzun, in a recent article, maintains that friendship between teacher and pupil is impossible. It is true, perhaps, in great classes, or in urban universities, where the classroom is the only contact, though even under such handicaps my father never found it so. In Europe official relations certainly discourage it. Perhaps Dr. Barzun is thinking of his own lycée days in France.

But certainly in America friendship is the indispensable atmosphere of a shared learning. I should not have wished to teach if it were not so. The authority of the older person, based on experience and wider study, need not prevent the shared life, if it is held in reserve as needed, and if teacher and pupil are both of the community of scholars.

My good friend Dr. John J. Moorhead, my brother John's classmate, and in 1915 a famous New York surgeon, jokingly predicted for me, knowing my hankering for friendship, a short and tragic end to my presidency. "You'll get in trouble with some girl," he said, "and there'll be an almighty bust-up. Better leave while all is serene."

Miss Jordan's parting advice to me had been "Keep a stiff elbow." I never found it necessary. Once only, a bold lass made a pass, on a bet, as I learned later. I was too dumb to notice it, she told me later, with chagrin. That side of college friendship did not come my way. It is not in the common American tradition, as the record of our education shows, though one would never guess it, to read our literature.

In my whole term no serious case of morals involved any man on our faculty. I had known two cases, one at Harvard, one at Smith. Under flagrant provocation there was some indiscretion, no doubt, but I did not hear of it. One kiss, benignly bestowed, almost cost one professor his job, but the trustee committee to which I referred his appeal was merciful.

My rashness was all of another kind. I was certainly impatient of restraint. One Sunday driving home from church, I found the college gate closed and, as I thought, locked. In a temper I drove straight through the side gateway of Taylor Hall, a feat which seems impossible today. Some good angel held my wheel, for on the other side stood Dean McCaleb. Had I scratched a stone of her beloved Dr. Taylor's hall, I should never have heard the last of it, until it had become the last of me.

Miss Ella McCaleb, of best Pennsylvania Scotch-Irish fiber, had come with President Taylor as his secretary and had been secretary of the college, and in 1913 dean of Vassar. She had all the virtues, and some of the failings, of the warm Ulster Scot: a temper, a love of a good fight, and then generous and fair dealing with her opponents.

What she had done, that she would do. So in my first days I found all my mail had been opened and read by the dean before I received it. In addition it seemed her prerogative to handle all general college correspondence. "What will the dean do to him?" asked my somewhat fearful sister-in-law, Marion Dodd, '03. The battle was short and sharp, and Miss McCaleb retired in good order. She kept her motherly hand on all the branches of her own work, however, and it was not easy to develop the bureaus of admission, of student employment, and of registry of marks, as they should be. Faculty action as well as my influence had to work by indirection before much was done.

For Miss McCaleb a good college meant a college of what she called "nice girls." She was right, I thought, in her emphasis on personality, but wrong in her choice of attributes. When the first group of students from Czechoslovakia were announced she came to me and said: "I will not have girls with such names in my college." Yet when they came, and one of them lost a parent by bereavement, it was Miss McCaleb who came to her and said: "My dear, you are coming to live with me for a time, until the pain is less."

So in the end the woman who had worked shoulder by shoulder with Dr. Taylor for thirty years came to work with me in a true friendship until her death.

———

The year wore on to its close, and every day helped me to make my decision. Because there was something I could do, I would stay. First of all, I laid the ghost of my inferiority complex about my predecessor. I could never be a Dr. Taylor. I lacked his gift of warm and full approach. Rich folk might be helped by me to see Vassar as object of their giving, but not for friendship's sake. The world of college presidents, in which he was an outstanding figure, I willingly renounced. New York club life, however helpful its contacts, was not for me. I tried them a while, dropping in when I could, but soon resigned.

The close, intense family feeling of loyalty could not be my contribution. That would always be Taylor's gift to the Vassar heritage, though not, I hoped, to the exclusion of wider loyalties. Perhaps I might help our students to look less in upon the college, and more out upon its world. They had always done this in some degree; my task would be to help in making it a central aim.

To put it in a phrase, I would try to make every Vassar woman a citizen of the world as well as of her college, state, region, or country. I would emphasize the international aspect of learning, by increasing the number of teachers of foreign birth, the number of foreign students, and the number of courses on international subjects. In doing this, however, I would not lose sight of the foreground of the Vassar scene. To be a citizen of the world, one must first be a citizen of somewhere. So, begin with Arlington. Let us cooperate with town government, help to get better highways, better schools, better health, by encouraging our faculty to lead in these movements. Poughkeepsie and Dutchess County would share in this effort. We would play fair with the city in our business relations, and try to eliminate town-and-gown tension once and for all. There was no place for it in a modern college. The index to Dr. Taylor's "Vassar" did not contain the word "Poughkeepsie." If I ever wrote a book about the college it would be found.

Indeed, I believed that the town and the county were Vassar's best and biggest laboratory, as New Haven should have been Yale's. There was not a science nor an art that could not profit by a better feeling and a closer tie. To take Vassar out of the classroom as I had taken my Beirut scholars a dozen years before, teaching the English language not from a book only, but from the life of the market and the olive orchard, was my ambition.

Vassar must be a better neighbor to her sister colleges. On the day after the Fiftieth Anniversary, President Burton of Smith, President Pendleton of Wellesley, and President Woolley of Mt. Holyoke met at my invitation in my office and organized the Association of Four Colleges. We did not dare ask Miss Thomas of Bryn Mawr. She would have haughtily refused. After Miss Thomas retired, however, Bryn Mawr joined, and so later did Barnard and Radcliffe. The old intimacy has been lost, but the cause of women's colleges has doubtless gained by the larger circle.

With these colleges Vassar would drop the old certificate system, and join men's colleges in trying to raise standards of admission by using examinations like those used in England. Under Miss McCaleb's management the admission was by school certificate only, the dean closing the list of applications whenever the list contained twice the number for which Vassar had room. By experience she had found that one-half would drop out, or fail to get the certificate. In 1915 the list was closed in the spring of that year, six months in advance. But by 1922 the list was closing *six years* in advance, so great was the increase in the number of applicants. This was due mostly to the war and to the Nineteenth Amendment, but also in part to the fact that more girls knew and liked Vassar.

The system broke down, and by degrees I was able to persuade the faculty and the trustees to abolish advance registration and open the college to a completely competitive system. Miss McCaleb dreaded the loss of the "nice girls," who would not pass those terrible examinations; she was happily disappointed. Any girl who really wanted to come could pass them. Entrance to Vassar was the choice of mature young women, not lassies of twelve years of age.

I would try to use the same system in college—to let a student study what she fitted herself to study, not to hedge her in with red tape. Upperclass students would be free to take long periods of independent study, using methods until then restricted to the graduate schools. They would be given credit for summer work carried on by themselves, alone or in groups, in connection with a favorite subject. We would look beyond marks to the student herself, not use them mechanically as disciplinary bars. If they had any value, which I was not prepared to debate, it was an educational value. Marks could perhaps show interest or ability, improvement in maturity. We would use them in this way.

Never again would I consent to use my authority as I had had to do in my first week at Vassar in dismissing twenty-three fresh- men in one day. We would abolish expulsion during the year, and at the year's end give every possible chance to the freshman who could show cause even with failing marks. Our standards would rise, not fall, I felt sure.

We would broaden Vassar's social rules. Some of them came down from the Victorian boarding schools. Professor Myra Reynolds, '80, my most delightful trustee and friend (*Learned Lady in England*, etc.), who was followed by Edith Rickert, '91 (*Chaucer*), in shedding luster on the University of Chicago for over forty years, assured me that in her dormitory supervision at that place of learning where young women came and went un- hampered by rules, the general social conventions and moral standards were as well upheld as at restricted Vassar, where she had taught from 1884 to 1892. Upon this testimony I determined to plump for freedom with responsible self-government. Young men were no longer restricted to Sunday calls. Chaperonage was no longer personal. When a girl eloped I was no longer asked to rush to the station to break up the match. It all came about as Miss Reynolds had predicted. So far as we knew, responsible student attitudes were far more effective in promoting reasonable standards of conduct than all the complicated system of rules.

The wardens, or house chaperones, who spent most of their day recording absences, could be far better employed as coun- selors. But to make them effective, training in guidance would be necessary, and this was not yet available. We had heard of mental hygiene, but did not yet think of it as valuable training for normal young people.

I began to refuse to carry out penalties left to my discretion to execute. I urged teachers to let up—I transferred to Student Government, with faculty approval, all responsibility for hon- esty in written work. In all this Professor Lucy Salmon was my unfailing support. "Call them women, not girls," she urged, "and you'll see that they will act like women." So I did, and banished the term "college girl" from my vocabulary. There were some, however, who still spoke of little darlings.

The broadening relations included the younger faculty, who were given the vote, placed on important committees, and generally treated as citizens. Employees came into the picture as human beings. Marjorie became their steadfast friend. Personal relations had always been kind at Vassar between individuals, but something was yet to be done to break down barriers of social caste and thoughtless neglect.

Would all this extension of relations at Vassar take away from standards of college work? On the contrary, as it turned out. The loss of time involved was more than made up by the heightening of interest. Dawdling was replaced by purposefulness, according to teachers' reports. Steadily year by year a higher number of students graduated, and fewer were dropped for failure. The general level of work improved, at least as far as the evidence of grades could be trusted.

In my New York speech I had said: "If you want students to respond to their opportunities at Vassar, make them responsible. There is no other way." There were moments of doubt, but my way was lighted by that belief.

MATTHEW VASSAR'S COLLEGE

THE BEST FRIEND I made that year was old Matthew Vassar himself. Looking around for something to read about the little college at the end of the trolley line I found that the man who knew most about it was the old brewer whose malt-houses once stood at the other end of the trolley, down by the river dock. In my enthusiasm for his story, I had a thousand postal-card views of the brewery struck off for visitors at the fiftieth anniversary that October. Unfortunately a Poughkeepsie trustee of the college was one of the first to be offered a card, and he promptly confiscated the lot.

This squeamishness about the source of Vassar's founding was of long standing. The students had been required to bowdlerize their song about the Founder:

> "Then here's to Matthew Vassar,
> Our love shall never fail,
> For well we know that all we owe
> To Matthew Vassar's ale."

"Fail" and "ale" were censored; "fade" and "aid" replaced them, and both song and aid faded soon away into the limbo of songs with no point.

Old Vassar had no squeams about it, I was glad to learn. When an admiring friend wrote to ask him the secret of his success, he replied: "My chief business for most of my life was with 'John Barleycorn, my Joe John.' "

47

Historically, I learned that whales as well as ales had something to do with Vassar's fortunes. Just up the river above the brewery, on the old map of Poughkeepsie which I hung on the wall outside my office, was the large dock of the Poughkeepsie Whaling Company, and under it "M. Vassar." The sweet summer breeze from the docks in 1830 must have been something.

Matthew Vassar was an Improver, to use the language of his day. He worked for a greater Poughkeepsie. The Savings Bank of which he was president was the second oldest in the state, and the first to be allowed to lend money on real estate mortgages. The fast-growing town was mapped out for lots far beyond its present streets, and the farm to which his father James Vassar retired was soon cut up in a sub-section.

Matthew was chairman of the committee of citizens which went to New York and borrowed money to build the first Hudson River Railroad, in days before Commodore Vanderbilt was interested. He built ships for his West Indian molasses at the Poughkeepsie shipbuilding dock below Kale Rock, just south of the brewery. The schooner "Matthew Vassar" was one of the fleet of blockaders off Mobile Bay during Farragut's days, and other Vassar boats are listed in the Navy of the Civil War.

On his desk at the brewery stood an old copper pitcher of ale for his refreshment, a memento preserved by his nephew Henry Booth, and presented by him to me. At one of the first Founder's Days I poured out some (ginger) ale and quoting Dogberry's toast "God save the Foundation" drank it off to the cheers of the students. The draught was almost fatal to my term of office. A New York newspaper noted the fact, and next day the Women's Christian Temperance Union raised the hue and cry for my scalp. I escaped by a hair.

I read all I could find about Matthew. Professor Elizabeth H. Haight of our Latin Department published his fragment of autobiography and some of his letters, mercifully preserved after the destruction of most of his records by ruthless heirs. Dr. Taylor had written with Miss Haight's aid a history of the college.

In his eagerness to prove Vassar's claim as the first women's college he had also compiled a book with the modest title "Before Vassar Opened." My quotations are often from these sources.

Prexy proved to his own satisfaction that the many colleges of the South, the early efforts of Mary Lyon at Mt. Holyoke, and even Elmira College, which predated Vassar's founding by a full ten years, were really of no importance. "Vassar really marked an epoch. Therefore to most the foundation seemed new, and the founder one of the great Originals." I found these claims to priority of little account. But the man who did the founding meant more than mere dates to his college, and I worked this vein with diligence. On a trip to England in later days I visited his birthplace, a few miles west of the sturdy town of Norwich, and found the old horse pond into which Matt fell as he rode the farm horse to water, and was pulled out half-drowned.

One day in June, 1940, I received a cable from England, signed Kathleen Vassar, addressed only to the college, and asking whether someone would take her little daughter as a refugee. My wife and I talked it over, and cabled back "send reference." Next day I got a cable which has always seemed to me a masterpiece of the British art of understatement. "Dear Christine is quite average. Signed, Headmistress."

That was enough. We cabled "send her along." By August she was with us; and Christine Vassar became a member of our family for the next eight years.

"Quite average" was good enough to land her as first in her class at the local high school, and sporting a Phi Beta Kappa key at a Vassar Commencement three years later. One year more at Columbia, with a fellowship, and the master's degree is to follow, when the thesis is finished, under the watchful eye of a professor at the University of London, Bedford College. Now she is back in the States, a statistical clerk in the office of population statistics at Princeton.

With her father, Walter Vassar, in 1946 I explored the family records, at the Genealogical Society, the British Museum, and in various towns and churches of Norfolk. We found the earliest notices in the Huguenot Church registers of Norwich. The Vassars were in Norfolk by 1550, refugees from persecution in France, and protected by Henry the Eighth. The East Anglians didn't relish the newcomers, and the king had to issue a royal order to the townsfolk to leave them alone. They brought to England new ways of weaving, and prospered. Soon Vassars, in various spellings (Vasser, Vasour, Vaseure, Vessure) began to appear in churchyards of neighboring towns, until down in Shipdham parish five of them, probably brothers, held farms. One of them was Matthew's grandfather, James, one was Walter's ancestor, Charles.

Two brothers in the next generation migrated in 1796, bringing substantial funds. Little Matthew was one of the children; more were to be born at Poughkeepsie, where the brothers purchased two hundred acres on the banks of Wappingers Creek. My wife and I now live on a farm whose northern line is the southern limit of the first Vassar farm. To the top of Sunrise Hill, where the farms edge each other, Matt climbed one day with his big sister Mary, and viewed the landscape o'er. Below him lay the Poughkeepsie fair grounds and race track, now the college campus. Beyond lay the town, with its steeples shining in the morning sun. With satisfaction he recalls this day in his autobiographical notes. Matt went to the races once in a while in later days, but prudently pulled down the curtains of his buggy, he tells us, so that the good townspeople would not see him on his way to the sink of iniquity.

Dr. Leroy Cooley, Vassar's first professor of physics, was a great friend of old Matthew, and inherited his gold-headed cane. From his son I received it as a personal gift, and I have given it to Sarah Blanding as a staff of office. On its gold cap is inscribed "Mary to Matthew, Christmas 1850." No doubt it was in honor of the famous walk the two children had taken fifty years before.

Another cane, or rather swagger-stick, has a more interesting history. Matt's schooling ended abruptly with the affair of the yellow breeches. His schoolmaster caned him one day, and the angry little boy let fly at him with his bottle of ink. The aim was true, and the dominie's yellow breeches were well spattered. Matt tells in his autobiography how he went home under another boy's greatcoat. No more school. He left, scarcely able to read; and his spelling was never better than that of the freshmen at Vassar, which is not saying too much, certainly. At fourteen years, the little boy ran away from home to seek his fortune. He would not agree to become a farmer's apprentice, as his father desired. So, with his mother's sympathetic aid, "to seek my fortune with 6/ in my pocket, two corse East India Muslin shirts, a pair of woolen socks, Scow Skin Shoes, all tied up in a Cotton Bandana Handkerchief," he walked to the ferry at New Hamburg, and kissed his mother goodbye.

Over a hundred years afterwards, a friend found in the Vassar garret in Poughkeepsie a boy's swagger-stick. On the silver cap were rudely scratched the initials "M.V." Into the top of the cap was pressed a silver sixpence, with the date upon it, 1805. Matt's hegira was in 1806. The swagger-stick was given me, and now serves as baton for the cheer-leader of the college from year to year when she leads her classmates in song.

Little by little we have been able to add to the portrait of Matthew Vassar first drawn by Dr. Taylor and Elizabeth Haight, until today the figure is the mental property of every Vassar girl. Nothing, I think, repaid the old man so much as the affectionate regard in which the students held him. With one of them, Sarah Stilson, he kept up a correspondence, which we published in 1915.

"The first Founder's Day was a most joyous occasion, with an arch of triumph, poems and songs and a royal feast." As the years passed, Founder's Day became rather stilted. A formal lecture was its chief event. It seemed to me that the old spirit of merrymaking was rather in line with Vassar's English origins and with his personal temperament. So today, after the march to Prexy's, and the brief words of welcome, into which I managed to weave something new each year from the Vassar tradition as it came to light, the day is a real holiday of sports, games, and plays, in which the college looks at itself in the best of humor.

Amusing is Vassar's entry in his diary concerning the death of his little dog Tip, who sits sedately in the full-length portrait of the Aula.

> Tuesday, Nov. 23, 1863. Tip taken quite sick last night with applexy wrote his Euolgy, expecting he will die before morning.
>
> Mon., Nov. 30. Gave poor dog Tip a dose of morphine shall know the results in morning
>
> Tues. Dec. 1. Poor Dog Tip died this morning He was drowned in the Brewery Cistern of the old Malt house and buried by Joseph Jarochs asside of Dog-Den in his Master'[s] garden I would not see the sight and therefore went with Edward Vassar and Mr. Hunter to clean up plots of Baptist Burial Grounds. Called on "Swan" this p.m. and gave him Obituary of Dog Tip to have published.

A copy of the obituary, Old Matt's only published work, is in our library.

Is there any known parallel to the deliberate search of Vassar for a worthy object of his benevolence? In 1845, he, with his wife Maria and his secretary, Cyrus Swan, set sail for Europe. While the ship "Northumberland" was waiting in harbor for a favorable wind, Vassar bought the painting of the vessel which now hangs in the library. Arriving in London, he hastened to view Thomas Guy's Hospital, erected by a merchant like himself, "in his lifetime," as the tablet records. Struck by the phrase, Matthew Vassar decided to do likewise. The message from Guy, whom Vassar believed to have been in his own family tree—his brother was John Guy Vassar—came directly home to him. Here he was, prosperous at fifty. Why not retire and devote himself to some equally worthy cause?

In Paris, he visited the most famous buildings of the time— the Tuileries, the Hotel de Ville, the Luxembourg. He purchased plans of the buildings and marked them in his own hand. These are now in our library. On his return he set about his new task. After ten years of study and correspondence, he decided upon a women's college. Dr. Taylor tells the story well. Matthew's nephews—Matt Jr. and John Guy Vassar—opposed him at first, and pleaded for a hospital like Thomas Guy's. But that remained for them to found: the Vassar Brothers Hospital, Poughkeepsie's pride. Matthew was set upon making the college. According to him, the first suggestion came to him in the course of purchasing the Cottage Hill Seminary for the use of his wife's niece, Lydia Booth. Her grave, on which stands a tombstone resembling a teacher's stand with an open book laid upon it, tells of the love of her pupils for her. Every Founder's Day the students decorate it.

Milo P. Jewett, a Baptist minister and educator, got into touch with Vassar over the sale of his niece's school, and finding him interested in the idea of the college, encouraged and sustained the old man in his plans. Dr. Taylor gives too much credit to Jewett for the general plan, however, for it is certain that Vassar was in correspondence with a number of educators whose ideas he valued equally. As Matt's fertile mind played with all sorts of new ideas Jewett did nothing but oppose them. Especially obnoxious to him were Vassar's plans for education of women by women. They parted company when, with a building still unfinished, the exasperated Jewett gave vent to his irritation in an unfortunate letter, calling the old man "more childish and fickle every day." Trustee busybodies laid the letter before Vassar, and the jig was up.

Jewett had been generously treated by the Founder. At his expense, Jewett spent a year in Europe, trying to get ideas to use in women's higher education. As women in Europe had no higher education, his trip was entirely fruitless, though no doubt it was a delightful holiday. One wonders why Jewett ever thought it worth while. Vassar's first architect, Tefft, was given a similar trip, and made some good designs, but died in Italy. His successor, James Renwick, architect of Grace Church and St. Patrick's in New York, followed the pattern of the buildings Vassar had seen in Paris.

Main Building, said to be the first heated by steam from a special plant outside the building, was unique in many ways. Its numerous firewalls and protected stairs, its division into central college, professors' residence in north and south "towers," and above all its inside bedrooms with windows opening on a hall, went just a bit too far in protecting the delicate females of the period from high winds and Paul Prys. But the hall is still in full use after eighty-five years, its brickwork sound and its timbers sturdy, insured for more than a million. Well did Vassar observe that the style "symbolized solidity and chastity."

Over its erection Vassar watched with devotion and anxiety. Authorities might quarrel over what should be taught; Matthew knew, at least, good building. That he got, as he watched through the anxious years of the Civil War, while his stocks went down and the prices of building went up, and his fortune seemed likely to be wasted. The contractor, Henry Harloe, whose son-in-law William M. Calder was in the Senate in 1915, went deeper and deeper in loss and finally went bankrupt, but Vassar kept on. Even a paralytic stroke did not deter him, though his doctor warned him not to become a slave to all his ideas.

Like the good businessman he was, he put his eggs in one basket, and watched that basket. He advertised widely the forthcoming opening of his college, circulating colored prints of the college, and buying space in magazines and newspapers. Consequently, and probably for the first time in educational history, Vassar College was crowded to the doors on its opening day, and students were turned away.

One of the disappointed ones, Mrs. D. M. Baker, told me that she applied too late, and as all rooms were full, she was allowed to sleep on the floor of one of the parlors. Frightened by mice, she climbed on top of the grand piano for the rest of the night. Next day, going back to town and lunching at Smith Brothers restaurant, she was picked up by a handsome young man, and incontinently married him. The offspring of this sudden rebound from college was Dr. Josephine Baker, the famous child specialist and director of Child Welfare in New York City.

"Saturday, January 30, 1864—My dear Wife Catherine Died this day one year ago at ¼ of 10 O.K. P.M." So runs the only entry in Vassar's quaint diary that refers to Catherine Booth. No recorded word of hers remains, but the student tradition tells that the only word she spoke, when her husband told her of his plan to build a women's college, was "Oh, Matthew!" Her portrait in Vassar parlor, and the lovely portrait of her niece Louisa van Kleeck Vassar (Mrs. M.V. jr.) in the blue parlor, show at least that there were ladies in Poughkeepsie in those days.

I might tell much more of Matthew, for the story keeps enlarging. His portrait as a youth of thirty I bought at an auction in Washington, and still possess. It was formerly the property of his nephew Edmunds, from the estate of whose sons the picture came up for sale. Edmunds had been financed by his uncle in a real estate speculation in what was then pioneer country in Michigan. This resulted in the settlement of the city of Vassar, Michigan, a thriving small town today. Edmunds was a delegate at the Republican Convention of 1860, and as a result, I suppose, of his services in the cause was rewarded by appointment to the office of Clerk of the Senate of the United States. This accounted for the portrait's trip to Washington.

During the four war years in which the college was a-building, the debate over the plan of study went on. Vassar's hopes for a practical education suited to women and taught by women was given up, and Jewett's scheme for a university course similar to that at Virginia, also went by the board. The plan adopted was of the standard type, but uncommonly free in its elective system, some years earlier than Eliot's at Harvard.

But here, at any rate, was a college started with a fully equipped library of 10,000 volumes; with fine "cabinets" of apparatus in all the sciences, and equipped laboratories in astronomy, physics, chemistry, geology, botany, and physiology; with a gallery of art, not too good, but including water colors of Turner bought from John Ruskin, which Ruskin afterwards vainly tried to retrieve. A whole battery of Steinway pianos enabled the young ladies to give a recital at Commencement playing twelve pianos at once. Here was the first gymnasium for women collegians, and the first regularly organized department of physical education at any American college, outdating Amherst. Here was a whole collection of conchology, the beginnings of a natural history museum unique among our colleges, and not surpassed today in some aspects by any college. For all this, and much more, the Founder paid during days of shrinking capital funds.

From these years of planning and carrying through his "great design" as Dr. Taylor calls it, Matthew Vassar evolved a simple philosophy of education and of life. His first basic idea was, that the best was none too good. Vassar College was to be abreast of all that was finest in American education. American women were to have a chance at an education equal in quality to any offered in institutions for men. From the first he issued this challenge. From this insistence, transmitted to his beloved students, came the traditions of a certain aggressiveness or forwardness in the Vassar temperament. Mt. Holyoke's fame for piety, Wellesley's for sweetness, Smith's for sociability, Bryn Mawr's for intellectuality, were matched by Vassar's fame for getting what she wanted.

When the humorous novelist Frank R. Stockton wrote his very popular story "Squirrel Inn" it was the Bryn Mawr graduate that held high the banner of mental supremacy, but the Vassar heroine, domestic, demure, and determined, that got her man. From the time of Frank Stockton to the present the Vassar girl has been the darling of fiction, right down to John Marquand's "Point of No Return."

When Vassar in 1920 challenged Colgate to a debate, and won it, its team were true daughters of the Founder, who did not believe in hiding his light under a bushel.

"Do all things interlectural and material the best and make your prices accordingly. . . . I go for the best means, cost what they may, and corresponding prices in return." Thus Matthew, out of his business experience. Vassar has taken this counsel all too literally, its charges for tuition being always near the top of the larger Eastern colleges. In the keen competition for endowment and buildings, Vassar has just managed to keep up with the foremost women's group.

Useful knowledge. "What is generally taught in schools tends about as much toward discipline, self-knowledge, self-preservation or complete living as the fact 'My neighbor's cat kittened yesterday.' We want more practical life invigorating knowledge." This was written to Edward Youmans, the famous editor of the Popular Science Monthly, who had just sent Vassar a copy of Herbert Spencer's "What Knowledge Is of Most Worth?" Vassar agreed with Youmans on the great value of science, and no arts college had started with so strong a staff of scientists. One of them, Orton, was the first American geologist in the Andes. He is buried on an island in Lake Titicaca, beneath a monument in Inca style erected by Vassar alumnae.

"I do go for joyous exercise in the open air." Vassar placed health first. He advocated a swimming pool at the site of Sunset Pond. He provided for rainy days, too. The corridors of Main, it is said, were planned not for protection of health, but to enable the young ladies, in inclement weather, to promenade past opened windows. Vassar urged swings. We may laugh, but there are swings and swings.

Art and music were to be given equality with other subjects.

At least one course in art was required of all students. The love of beauty was still further encouraged by the requirements that each student was to have her own plot of ground in the Floral Circle, and cultivate it with an eye to design.

Modern languages were from the first given equality with classical languages. How rare this was in 1865 may be seen in a pamphlet in Mr. Vassar's book collection at the library by the professor of English at the University of Pennsylvania, Henry Coppée. He argued for modern languages and science in a commencement address at Gettysburg College in 1859, that "The sole object of university education is to fit men for life here and life hereafter."

"You had the ancient classics; give them now their just due; but here are the modern classics. Will you not study them?"

"We are told long and earnest study of Latin and Greek train the mind. So it does; but I say train it in part by studying modern languages. . . ."

Only one classical language was required for entrance. Greek was not taught at first. This was a deliberate halving of the standards at men's colleges. By some taken as a sign of inferiority, it was really a step in the right direction. Students, better prepared than ever, can enter now with no requirement of Latin.

Originality. "If we only do what others have done we are imitationists, not progressionists. My motto is Progress." I chose this last as the title of an early commencement address, in a plea for a truly liberal college. I told how Matthew Vassar had pleaded so hard, in his retiring speech as chairman of his board, for a new building to be devoted to the science of Household Economy, that his heart failed him, and he sank back in death before the startled trustees. It took fifty years, and the devoted labors of a trustee, Minnie Cumnock Blodgett, before Vassar's wish was gratified. But Vassar's speech was the original source.

What Vassar was after, and what I found to be my own inspiration, was the idea that while liberal arts education is not to be primarily determined by the sex of the student, yet there are areas of special interests reserved by custom of sex. Child study and sociological studies of the family ought to be pursued by both sexes, but as a matter of fact women elect the courses, men do not.

In other words, the consideration of women as women, of life in the family, wifery, housewifery, maternity, nutrition, the arts and sciences of the home, are natural introductions to the fields of biology, political science, law, and morals, where women are the students.

It was a bitter blow to some of Vassar's professors when euthenics, the science and art of human welfare, was formally adopted in 1924 by faculty and trustees, and the first child study major in an American college of arts was authorized. Yet over a hundred years ago Count Rumford bequeathed to Harvard a professorship in the art of living.

"You are driving women back into the home, from the slavery of which education has helped us to escape, Dr. MacCracken," cried Professor Margaret Washburn. I could sympathize with her, for she had fought valiantly in that battle for recognition. But now the battle was won, and only a cleaning up campaign was needed. The door was open, even if only on a crack, to the halls of the learned professions. Women, having reached this point, were turning around in thousands, and saying, "But look, I want to marry and have children. I want a better life for them than children have had hitherto; better health, better homes, better lives in all ways, material and spiritual. Is it an art or a science to tell how this can be done? Whatever it is, I want it."

All this was in Vassar's mind. He wanted a college of women for women. He did not get it, partly because there were at the time not enough trained women to create the college, partly because his advisers were mostly men.

"Nothing is so much trouble in my apiary as the confounded old drones," wrote Matthew. "They will neither work nor let anybody else."

Matthew's entomology may not have been very scientific, but he had something. Until women led women the fight was not won. That is why I rejoice that my successor is a woman.

It was Matthew Vassar's influence that secured Maria Mitchell for the Vassar faculty and brought fame to the first woman professor of great note in America. Helen Wright's fine biography "Sweeper of the Skies" tells the whole story of opposition to the appointment by the college staff, of lowering the salary far below that offered men, and of Miss Mitchell's courageous choice. As the storm center of liberalism on Vassar's early campus, when Elizabeth Cady Stanton could speak only in Miss Mitchell's private rooms, and Louisa Alcott was a dangerous radical to all except Miss Mitchell, the little Quaker lady fought a valiant battle for freedom of the mind.

Over the entrance to Vassar's Main Building ran the legend:

Vassar Female College
M. Vassar Founder, 1861.

The word female was a fighting word in those days. To most men it was a word of indifferent significance. To women it meant all that was bestial, or servile, in their lot. The cow, the sow, the hen, were females. *They* were women, and meant to be treated as such, not as chattels.

Sarah Closser Hale, editor of Godey's Lady's Book, was the leader in this fight. The U. S. census still classifies men and women as male and female, so does the passport division, but elsewhere you do not meet the word once in a month of Sundays. That is Mrs. Hale's doing. You may smile at it now, but it took courage then.

Mr. Vassar had been misled by the custom of his day, and Mrs. Hale undertook to set him right. A long correspondence ensued, and shortly the people of the State of New York passed a law abolishing the word in the college charter. Mr. Vassar was able to write Mrs. Hale that the hated word was removed forever from Vassar College. This, in spite of President Raymond and all his sound reasoning in defence of the word. He defended "Female" because already it was "Elegantly lettered in massive stone," "in characters of gold on a pure white marble tablet."

It would require an act of the legislature to remove it. Addressing himself to the main argument, and quoting the Biblical "male and female created he them," he admitted that the primary meaning is "to distinguish sex, and that only," but argued that a secondary meaning "pertained to persons of that sex," and that in this sense "Female schools, female seminaries, female gymnasiums, and female colleges are to be found wherever the English language is spoken."

"Simplicity, euphony, convenience," all these the term possessed. "Ought not all these considerations to outweigh even a somewhat serious objection of mere taste—an objection felt only by a few of unusual refinement?"

In red ink, on the margin of this letter, is a note in Mrs. Hale's hand: "It has been done."

"The truth is it is all nonsense and irreconcilible with Divine truth in regard to the Mental Capacity of women, nothing but long prejudice with the domineering spirit of Man has kept Woman," etc. Matthew Vassar believed in suffrage.

In accordance with this opinion, which few men held in 1865, Vassar began to entrust his beloved institution to the women in his student body. On the second Thanksgiving he wrote to them:

"I deeply regret that my health will not permit my joining them today. I wanted to say to them, that, the "Vassar College" is now *thiers*, *thiers* to elevate, *thiers* to beautify, *thiers* to honor, and *thiers* to adorn, by its fruits, and I trust God in his Providence will bless, prosper, and sustain it." How radical this statement was only educators know. What? A college belong to its students? Never. To the trustees? Yes, legally. To the faculty? Yes, practically. But Matthew actually believed in young people and in trying new ways. "While the hoary head is often the seat of wisdom, it is not allways the vehicle for great mental action. It takes 'Young America' to be the pioneer of progression, the fathers to hold on to the old homestead."

"I am perfectly aware of my ignorance to lead, and perhaps my folly even to suggest anything new—yet relying upon a long life of observation and experience in the common business affairs of the world I may have gathered up some knowledge that may have escaped thro' their apparent insignificiency the minds of the more learned."

The tyranny over the college student is the greatest anomaly in education. Vassar struck it off at one blow. His influence has helped ever since to set his students free. When the unknown giver of Students Building created a center for student extra-curricular life, she (if she) stated that the building was to belong to the students association, to be under its control, its endowment fund managed by students. This is only one of many instances in which Vassar students have taken Matthew Vassar at his word. The old traditions of college as a nursery for the immature girl soon covered the clearing which Vassar had started in the academic grove. The generous vistas were lost as the grove grew higher, and many of the older alumnae told me of their discontent with the restricted life that they led. Harriot Stanton Blatch, Gertrude Mead, and Belle Skinner were some of these. They were not reconciled to their college until they learned that a new freedom had come along Matthew Vassar's lines.

In a letter to his loyal nephews, urging them to stand by, he wrote: "The great beauty of my idea is its unlimited expansion . . . When I contemplate it my mind falls into an ecstasy."

In his last year of life, Vassar designed his own tombstone. When it was erected he invited the students to come down and view it. Before the assembled group the pawky little old man in the towering silk hat smiled and said, as he laid his hand upon the gigantic granite acorn: "Young ladies, I hope you catch the idea."

They caught the idea. They spread Vassar's English oakleaf in their designs. But they themselves have become, as he intended, the great oak grove that has sprung from the sound English acorn that was the Founder. The tall oak groves on Sunrise Hill are symbols of Vassar's spirit.

THE FACULTY INTIME

WHY DOES THE COMMUNITY OF SCHOL-
ARS hold so little in common? Why does each scholar bear the
company of others reluctantly, and scatter each to his cell at
the first release? The question is something musty.

In "Religio Magistri," an *Atlantic Monthly* essay which I
wrote soon after coming to Vassar, I set forth that the good
teacher believes in his subject, in his scholar, and in himself.
Students were fired by the burning enthusiasm of their teacher
for the subject taught. They would forgive almost any lack but
that.

But the same zeal that inspires the teacher may not make for
harmony in faculty life, if it is pushed to excess, for then intolerance accompanies it.

> For virtue, growing to a pleurisy,
> Dies in his own too much.

At Harvard I knew, as all other students did, about the quar-
rels in the Harvard faculty. W. A. Neilson never disguised his
active contempt for W. H. Schofield, the playboy of the English
teachers. Copeland admitted he was in the doghouse because
he insisted that poems were meant to be read aloud rather than
studied. Intolerance is the faculty hot sauce.

At Yale I knew A. S. Cook's isolation in an unhappy eminence of Anglo-Saxon scholarship. I had known the hostility of
some of my colleagues, when in an unlucky moment I ventured

the suggestion that the Graduate Students Club should be allowed to run itself without interference from the professors. I never recovered from the shock. Once I went in my discomfiture to Uncle Toby Cross, my departmental head, for consolation. He said: "Noble, you'll just have to learn that there are people who dislike you, and get along with the knowledge as well as you can. You can't be friends with everybody."

When Tucker Brooke, my warm friend of Oxford days, had come to Yale on my recommendation and was in danger of being dropped from the faculty after his first not too successful year, my interference with a plea for him met with keen resentment. So I knew something about tensions within the charmed circle of academic life. I was not prepared, however, for the intricacy or the intensity of such problems at Vassar. On the second day of my term there entered my office Miss Abbie Leach, Professor of Greek, bearing a satchel which she emptied upon my desk.

"These documents," she said, "constitute the basis of my charges against Miss Macurdy, the other member of my department."

It had all begun, apparently, with an iota subscript. Miss Leach, entering Miss Macurdy's classroom one day, had found upon the table some corrected papers. She glanced at them, and was horrified to see that her colleague had failed to correct the missing iota in a masculine dative. That was enough. From that time she had been certain that Grace Macurdy was no scholar.

I stood up, gathered the papers solemnly, replaced them in Miss Leach's bag, and placed it by her side.

"Miss Leach, take back these papers, and never let me see or hear of them again. My administration began yesterday. It will never review what happened yesterday or the day before that. Any attempt to the contrary will entail the most serious consequences."

There was a moment tense with electric frequencies in the academic air. Miss Leach looked ready to explode. Then the air cleared, and ozone could be sensed.

"At least we know where we stand," she said, and departed. I never heard the subject mentioned again by her.

Not that the matter was ended. When I recommended Grace Macurdy for promotion, as I did at the end of the semester, it was without Miss Leach's approval. In its place, I had a dozen letters from scholars of equal eminence in the faculty. Miss Macurdy won her way to eminence as a scholar, writer, and teacher, and today is remembered as one of the most distinguished professors in Vassar's long list. Her wonderful collection of Greek art is now a part of Vassar's Classical Museum.

Let it be said at once that Miss Abbie Leach was also a distinguished woman and teacher of no common quality. After her death I recognized it by placing her name on a tablet in Vassar's memorial hall as one of five famous scholars in the earlier days of the college, and as the "nucleus" of Radcliffe College. Her insistence on instruction in classics had been the agent that mobilized the women who won Harvard's reluctant consent to its "Annex." To her further credit be it recorded, that when she knew of her own mortal illness, she arranged to pay a formal call upon Miss Macurdy in her chambers, and drank the tea of reconciliation with her. It was a heroic act, worthy of Thermopylae.

Two days after the encounter with Miss Leach, Miss Lucy Salmon, famous head of Vassar's History Department, came in with a similar complaint against Dean McCaleb. More voluble than Miss Leach, she was harder to cork, but I managed at last, with more rudeness, I am afraid, to drive in the stopper. I would not listen to a word of it. It was long before she forgave me.

She was not too easy in social ways. At our first reception to the faculty, she blocked the whole line with an interminable discussion, and finally pulled me out of the receiving party altogether, to continue it. This was too much for Marjorie, whose patience gave out. She stood up bravely to the redoubtable professor, and I came meekly back to the appointed task of shaking hands.

Not long after that Marjorie had a quite unintentional revenge. She invited Miss Salmon and Mr. Mills to the same dinner party, and placed them next each other, blithely unconscious that they had not spoken to each other for years. Back in 1890 economics had been started at Vassar as a branch of history, with Mr. Mills in charge. This separation of the two subjects was fiercely contested by Miss Salmon, and the controversy had lasted twenty-five years. But Marjorie's innocence turned the trick, and the embarrassed professors, feeling all eyes upon them, were forced into polite conversation. The awful moment passed without fisticuffs.

This was not the only conflict between woman and man in the faculty, as I was soon to learn. Some of them were caused by the man's attitude. George Shattuck, Professor of Geology, was a magnificent physical figure. He had been, while at Amherst, intercollegiate champion in the half-mile run, and there was about him always an air of abounding animal vigor, intolerable to some of the quiet, tired ladies of the faculty. His temperament, however, belied his physique. He suffered from lack of competitive life, and became a kind of chaperon, trying to protect tender females from the rough side of life. The females might be tender, but they resented his escort.

One of my first sights was a scene at the door of Main. Out from its portal came Miss Macurdy, dressed for a suffrage parade in Poughkeepsie, and proudly wearing a silk band across her bosom, emblazoning the awful suffrage colors, and *Votes for Women* shamelessly displayed. Mr. Shattuck met her. "I implore you, Miss Macurdy," he cried, "Don't go down there among that rough crowd. It isn't safe. You will be assaulted. You don't know what may happen."

"Out of my way, Mr. Shattuck," cried the embattled Amazon, and off she marched.

The men of the faculty numbered about a quarter of the whole body, and nearly all of them were heads of departments. Naturally, therefore, in this women's college there ensued a strife of the insubordinate bloc against the imposed domination of the male.

Sometimes the unexpected self-assertion of women professors came from the same dynamic that makes professors absent-minded—devotion to truth in one's special field. Among my best friends on the faculty was Miss Martha Beckwith, who held at Vassar the chair of Folklore, a rare if not unique position. In her researches she had lived with Hawaiians of the older stock, Negroes in Jamaican highlands, and reservation Indians.

"Come, Miss Monnier," she said one day. "The paper advertises a genuine Hawaiian hula at the theater. I want you to see it. A car just went by with a big poster, too. Genuine hula, think of it!"

Miss Monnier's protests were of no avail. Off they went to the theater on Main Street. At the door the usher asked for tickets. "Nonsense," said Miss Beckwith, "I am an authority." Awed and puzzled, the doorman let them through. They marched down to a central seat. The vaudeville was on, and the "hula" girls, from West Forty-second Street of course, capered on.

"This is unscholarly," said Miss Beckwith, "I must protest."

"Please, Martha, don't make a scene. What is the use?"

Martha Beckwith arose and addressed the audience. "In the interest of truth," she said, "I must denounce this performance. It has nothing about it that in any way represents the true hula except the skirt, and even that is artificial. You are being taken in."

The theater was in an uproar. "Go ahead, old lady. Speak your mind. Tell us about the hula! Sit down!" Miss Martha did not sit down. She told them what the true hula was, until the petrified manager came to life, and started off the "hula" once more.

"Come, Mathilde," said the scholar. "We will not stay for such an unscholarly performance."

Miss Monnier followed Miss Beckwith's stately withdrawal while the customers cheered.

Sometimes woman's aggression came from the sudden recognition of newly acquired powers. A young instructor one evening returned from her last lesson in judo in the faculty recreation class. At the door of Main Building she was accosted by a man who was waiting in the darkness. The thought flashed: "my judo." She extended her hand which the surprised stranger grasped. A quick turn, a powerful yank, and the stranger went flying over her head and into a big barberry bush which flanked the walk. Our heroine dashed for the door and got safely in.

"But did he speak to you?"

"Oh yes, something about how to get a taxi."

That's all there is. It is however pleasing to dwell upon the feelings of the stranger as he withdrew from the bramble bush, no doubt with his eyes scratched in again.

One of the kindest and most generous of the men, walking with me round the flower circle one evening improvised this parody:

"What though the Easter breezes
Blow soft round Vassar's pile
Where every prospect pleases
And only *man* is vile."

He soon after sought and found an excellent post at a men's college.

In general, the men in self-defense became conservative, opposing every change, while a triumphant women's majority drove them from pillar to post in faculty reform. Departments with women heads sought to keep men from any posts in their field, and the men in return, notably in art and music, added men to their staff as time went on. I could not honestly recommend a man to apply for a place in any department headed by a woman.

Conflicts within departments were often the result of some sex antagonism. A woman who sought the favor of the masculine was pretty sure to incur the hostility of the other women, and was likely to lose her post when the man retired. One department was so split over this that no meeting of its members could take place, and I was forced to assume a temporary chairmanship to enable them to organize. Men by themselves were not wholly free from such squabbles. In the gentle subject of philosophy the temperamental differences of the two men were so acute that they never spoke to each other.

In three departments the man-woman tension led to a splitting of the departments into two independent ones where the subjects of instruction permitted it. Thus geography was separated from geology and became a social science, and botany left the shelter of zoology. Unhealed splits occurred in other departments which remained united in name only.

Faculty tensions were no joke, however. At times I began to feel as if war would break out any minute on the campus, as it threatened to do upon the national scene that spring. I was led to study the causes of all these tensions, and to try whether through changes in the way of living, some improvement might not follow in human relations. Occasionally, in later years, marriage solved the problem most happily, as when Professor Philip Davis married Professor Hallie Flanagan.

But the chief cleavage did not run along the sex line. The academical animal, it seemed to me, was rather sharply divided into two groups. The first group, and the more numerous, might be called the analytical. Its nature was reflective, studious, industrious, but not dynamic. It sought a leader and was content to follow guidance. It was disinclined to physical exercise. Poor health often dogged such teachers, and timidity and inferiority controlled their feelings. They tended towards group life, since low spirits love company. They worked well in chosen grooves, preserving the great tradition of learning, but they would never add much to it, or alter its course.

The other group might be called creative. They were active, independent, aggressive. They exercised, and had a surplus of energy with which to combat disease. They led faculty action, and loved the scent of battle. The college was too small a field for them. They left the protection of college rooms, and lived in town, where they participated strénuously in civic life. They worked for suffrage, against child labor, against economic inequality and other forms of injustice. It was whispered of one of them that she had defended the right of an unmarried woman to bear a child and rear it. One or two, it was darkly hinted, were socialists. One even dared to be a Unitarian. Dangerous women, all of them. They rejoiced in every conflict of ideas. The times were ripe for change. One of them, Miss Washburn, had been intrepid enough to invade the sacred precinct of the men's smoker at psychological meetings. Marching uninvited into its midst, she had sat down and lighted a cigar. None questioned her privilege to enjoy the smoker thereafter.

When war came, Lily Taylor, a younger teacher of classics, went to Italy for the Red Cross, and worked there and in Yugoslavia. Another Latinist, Elizabeth Haight, chairmaned American studies in Rome, and became preëminent as an authority on classical narrative.

The creative group was as a whole superior to its station, the analytic group in danger of submitting to its handicaps. For the first my task seemed to be to further their projects, and support them with college funds or by special solicitation of aid. Thus, for the painter Chatterton, it was my task to find the money for a studio attached to his home. But it was the large group of analytics that became my particular charge. They were not all women, by any means. Indeed, in a college for women, the men who accepted posts were likely to leave soon for other fields if creatively disposed, leaving the analytics to carry on.

As I studied the situation, I found much in the college life that tended to worsen the status of the less active group. Whether they made the conditions, or the conditions made them, was of no consequence. A change was indicated as the treatment. The monotony of long years of teaching the same subject at the same dead level must be done away. One must have time to keep up to date. Either by shifting to new courses, or by introducing new methods of instruction, the pure waters of learning must be freed from the sludge brought down by the years. The long-studied private enterprises of research once started in high hope, but laid on the shelf for lack of encouragement, must be brought out and dusted. Grants for further study, for research, travel, and publications must be sought. The tired teacher must be made to feel that her college, with all its resources, was behind her and her own advancement.

So, when the time came to make an academic statute and to define the duties of the president, I wrote: "The function of the president is to conduct the administration with the purpose of advancing the interests of every department." I know of no better way of putting it; but I might add "and every teacher," which is tautologous but a little clearer.

To the teacher whose mind is centered on the relation of the college toward herself instead of her own impact on her world, nothing is so disappointing as the slow rate of promotion and increase of pay. By taking a personal interest in the teacher, by pointing out the relation between activity and promotion, and often by suggesting a subject of study and the means of securing time for it, I was able to give the lift needed to the discouraged worker.

Many scholars of the analytic type have a good deal of the creative quality undiscovered. To probe for this and find it became my work. To imbue every teacher with a sense of responsibility not only for her courses but for the whole college was the first step. To accomplish this meant an early extension of faculty suffrage. The younger instructors became voting members, and were added to important committees. I lived to see the time when the most vital faculty debates were led by a young instructor, who stood up to the Dean in open debate.

The decentralization of administrative work throughout the college, so that each teacher had an increased sense of her own value to the college, was the aim. I cannot say that it was ever fully attained, or that it was done quickly, but at least the centralizing tendency was checked. I tried my best to make a place in the work for the younger colleagues, and got a rich return in suggestions and cooperation.

The faculty as a parliament sat in an impossible room. It was on the third floor of old Main, given them because no one else wanted it. Dark and unventilated with two windows in corners, it was crowded when a hundred teachers met there. We moved to a lecture room in "Rocky," and as soon as it was possible, to the Aula, a hall of height and light, with comfort and dignity. It seemed to me, perhaps fancifully, that the quality of faculty debate became less bitter, more worthy of its nature, than in the old pesthole of a room, now made over into storage closets.

As individuals, the teachers had had but little care given them. To induce men with families to accept faculty posts, and to bring them into closer contact with the college, the trustees had constructed four houses for them, opposite the entrance on Raymond Avenue. Some devoted alumnae built a home for the librarian, Miss Wood, and others gave a home for Dean McCaleb. Dr. Hill built his own home on good terms, engaging to bequeath it to the college. This started a new plan, by which teachers could build their homes, selling them to the college on severance of the relationship by death or resignation. Three houses had been built under this plan. Further encouragement of it, in many cases by joining the college in the mortgage, has led to the erection of more than thirty houses by men and women of the faculty, on college land, at no rental fee. No house has been bought at less than original cost. Several of them are really two-apartment dwellings for the residence of two single teachers.

Fifty of the older teachers, all unmarried women, lived in single rooms in the student residence house. For them two apartment houses, Williams and Kendrick, were later built, the plans for them being started at once. Each was run on a club plan.

Other smaller apartments were purchased. Garden plots were offered and eagerly exploited.

There was scarcely a single private office in Vassar for any of its teachers. My activity in hunting for unused space led for a time to the nickname of "Attic Philosopher." The search was long and toilsome, but well rewarded, some fifty offices being added here and there. New buildings for various sciences met the scientists' needs pretty well. With the removal of five of the larger departments from Rockefeller Hall, its overcrowded rooms and offices were found adequate for the rest.

When the chance came to add space in the library, twenty-five research studies were built for faculty use. These rooms, with an occasional borrowing of the larger student cubicles, have greatly improved the facilities for scholarly work.

These are prosy details, but the planning and labor that went into their competition was fully compensated for by the appreciation of those for whom I worked. It meant much to me that Professor Washburn, probably our most famous scholar and certainly our best lecturer, could at last have her own building when the Vassar Brothers Laboratory was vacated by the Physics Department.

"Miss Washburn, do you feel easy in conscience?" I asked her, when she sat at ease in her new Zion. "This building is limited by deed of gift to physics and chemistry, you know."

"Certainly," said she. "After all, psychology is just a kind of physics. It is a mode of motion."

Vassar Brothers Laboratory is no more. A trustee skilled in engineering reported against it, and the old hall was torn down, while Blodgett received the psychologists in fireproof quarters. But that was after Miss Washburn's death. She would have resigned before accepting quarters designated under the general name of euthenics. Once, while playing golf with her over the new golf course on Sunset Hill, I remarked to her, not without a spice of malice, "What a beautiful view of Blodgett you get from here."

"I never look at it," she solemnly replied.

Miss Washburn's creative life led to research in science, but she stopped short of its application. Yet she freely granted that from applied science came much new evidence which theoretical science must take into account. It was just not her duty to use it, and she feared lest students of applied science would be stifled by its routine, and lose their divinely given intellectual curiosity.

With all this work for the bettering of conditions, and with all these efforts to make work at Vassar more attractive. I never succeeded in eliminating faculty tensions. Some folks just do not like others. I came to two conclusions in the final consideration. The first is, that tension is inherent in intellectual life, when workers live too much to themselves. The mutinous emotions, left to themselves in the preoccupation with the intellect, take their revenge in breaking down the restraints which life in a wider community enforces! Lifelong association, at very close quarters, is not easy at best, as all apartment house tenants well know. Unlikenesses and inequality of abilities tend toward friction, which a common love of scholarship does not succeed in overcoming.

Only something as strong as a common religion can remove it; and even religion has not made monastery or convent life ideal, if we can trust the witness of their chronicles. Man was not meant to live alone, but it should be added that women were not meant to live together. Nor men either.

VASSAR'S DARLING DAUGHTERS

THE DISTINCTIVE FEATURE of Vassar student life in 1915, which marked it at once from any college community I had known, was its creative gaiety. The great world war had darkened the horizon, but skies were still sunny overhead. College was made for good times. The faculty had not pushed the "work week" up to forty-five hours; they were content to get thirty hours at best. There was time for the exercise of originality.

The weekly exodus did not exceed a tenth of the students. That left a college on the campus, with recreation to be had by using its wits. It meant bacon bats on Sunset Hill, picnic bikes and hikes everywhere over Dutchess County's pretty hills, climbs up the Catskill paths, bird walks and botanizing, geology trips so leisurely—and so costly—that geology students were called "the idle rich."

It meant parties innumerable in student rooms, to which teachers were frequently invited. Stunts, impromptu dramatics, charades, and rhymes featured the fun that followed.

They studied once in a while, of course. Some students thought life was a bit too social, and pleaded for some way of keeping visitors out. For them I devised the "oak," borrowing the custom from sporting the oak door at Oxford. It was gratefully received by some, but did not sensibly diminish the sociability.

The "doorblocks," pads suspended on bedroom doors to receive messages when the occupant was absent or oak-bound, in-

75

vited scribbles in rhyme, and for a time doorblocks flourished as a type of occasional verse. Some of them were so witty that they were preserved in student albums and memory books. I once offered a prize for the best doorblock, and John Livingstone Lowes of Harvard not only was good enough to act as judge, but came to college and delivered his famous essay "The Fine Frenzy and the Quiet Eye." Much of it later appeared in his great book "The Road to Xanadu."

Vassar was a singing college. Step singing, borrowed like the senior song and a good deal else from Princeton, flourished on "Rocky's" steps in springtime. Marching songs were heard nightly as some group went by. Serenades under dorm windows echoed through the quads. A song contest at Founder's Day gave prizes for the best Alma Mater, the best comic song, and the best choral singing of some chosen classic. The entire college turned out, and excitement was intense. Mrs. Mary Thaw Thompson, a popular trustee whose daughters had led music at college, gave a beautiful silver cup as prize to the winning class. New songs sprang up from nowhere, and spread round campus almost daily. Songs at mealtime were as common as in a summer camp. The alma mater and marching songs of today were products of this spirit. Every class had its own song-book, with over a hundred songs of its own composition.

There was the same exuberant originality in art. Dorothy Walworth exploited her freshman course in Livy by designing a comic strip three inches wide and twelve feet long, containing ancient Rome's whole history in comic vein. It was so good that Professor Paul Shorey of the *Classical Journal* reviewed it favorably, noting that much credit was due the young artist, "Miss Pinxit D. Walworth." "Pink" got a nickname out of the editor's forgetfulness that Pinxit means "depicted."

Cartoons filled my mail. Pasquils and satire were pasted on so many places that professors began to complain. When the "scribbles tree" on the way to Rocky was cut down, I set up a bulletin board in Main Corridor, labelled "Pasquino," and for years it served as a safety-valve for student humor.

Vassar has always been stagestruck. In accordance with the practice at men's colleges of the day, the students were encouraged to form a literary society, good Matthew himself including a room for it in his Calisthenium. The room is now the Classical Museum. The speakers' platform was soon transformed into a stage, and the Philalethean Society gave up its pursuit of Truth (Alethea) in other ways than drama, and the plays in Philalethean Hall became known as Hall plays. Its "men" were garbed in black shirts, but allowed to wear whiskers. Not till years later were the plays opened to the general public. The Open Air Theater, built for the 50th Anniversary, and its superb Pageant of Athena has for thirty years dictated the choice of Third Hall and Class Day plays. The most striking performances were the cooperative alumnae-faculty-staff-student pageants, performed in the Open Air Theater once in four years. The "Pageant of Athena" was followed by "Kenilworth Revels," "Canterbury Tales," "Lorenzo de Medici," and other productions, written and produced by students with casts running up into the hundreds. Notable was the Alumnae play in 1921, Vincent Millay's "The Lamp and the Bell," written on the theme of woman's friendship for women. "If that is amateur acting, let me never be cursed with professional," said my brother-in-law Lee W. Dodd, himself a dramatist.

A play production by the English Department, later by the whole Faculty Women's Group, was given each spring for the senior class only. Its doors were sacredly guarded. There the dignified ladies disported themselves in tights. Marjorie, a capital actress, was recruited for a part in Jonson's "Eastward Ho!" To see her act, I tried to crash the gate, dressed as an old lady, but Warden Palmer's tearful prayers, asking me to think of the scandal if it should be known, made me desist. Shortly after, these plays were transferred to Founder's Day, and given for the whole college community.

In the heyday of the theater, Vassar had at least a play a week. Philaletheis, with a huge budget, produced three Hall Plays and two "minor Halls." Each House put on its own "one-acters" and "interludes" in the House parlors. Each department of language put on at least one play, while English classes chose scenes from Shakespeare. Music did a puppet play from Mozart. Classes in Dramatic Production (D.P.) acted at least three plays a year, with minor "Rehearsals" now and then. The faculty loved the theater so much that it frequently acted in student plays. On Founder's Day groups in the Floral Circle acted burlesques and the faculty put on its best play at eight.

Not content with this, the *Miscellany News* set up a "party" which soon became dramatic vaudeville. Dorothy Stockbridge, without benefit of faculty, boldly set up her own "Stockbridge Stocks," writing and producing her own plays. This little company, to which men recruits were added, continued as a semiprofessional company for some years in New York. After Stockbridge came OMGIM in "Scotty" Fitzgerald's day. (Oh My God, It's Monday!)

Add to them the Soph and Junior "Parties"—musical comedies in which practically the whole class rehearsed for weeks— and the wonder is that any work was done in other subjects. There was great complaint of sleepy eyes in studios and labs. Students first then petitioned for club chairs in the Libe. The Dean waged open war on D.P., and a great reform set in. Meanwhile from other colleges came the query: "What has happened at Vassar? We can't get our students to attend a college show."

All this activity was bound to lead to academic recognition. Vassar was lucky enough to have the right woman on her staff to pioneer. Gertrude Buck, Professor Wylie's associate, spent a sabbatical year at George P. Baker's Workshop 47 at Harvard, and on her return started a course in playwriting in 1916. Four years later she founded the Poughkeepsie Community Theater, which continued after her too early death in 1925. She was my warm friend, and the Gertrude Buck Fund for books in drama commemorates our friendship. The Vassar Theater which she had planned soon became a magnet of student enthusiasm.

On the dramatic wave, surfriding, came Hallie Flanagan, following Gertrude Buck's inspiration as a pupil of George Baker. To the love of acting she added an intellectual criticism and a social drive, making us believe that we could not only think in terms of theater, but that the theater was the natural vehicle for confronting the community with the facts of the time. It was daring. For a few years the Broadway critics came up to Vassar and wrote up its shows.

All this creative life was bound to experience a cyclical decline. It led, however, very naturally to a reform in the curriculum. Students were not satisfied with the results of their talent. They wanted to know more about art. So, as a result of student demand, courses in painting, piano and violin, play production and acting, were introduced, at first with little or no credit "toward the degree," later with a fair allowance in time and credit. Original composition in all fields was also recognized as college work. The change came first in the women's colleges. It has certainly raised standards of work in these fields, and provided professional material.

There was something electrical about Hallie Flanagan's directing. It was most rewarding to work in her productions, for the students and scarcely less for the few members of the faculty who enjoyed acting. Her book "Dynamo" (1943) tells the story of a genuinely experimental theater to which the whole college turned for intellectual stimulus.

She experimented in form, in historical revival, and in current issues; in original student plays and in the original Greek. In every performance at least one other department lent its aid, often half a dozen.

I had always loved to act. My wife's brother, Lee W. Dodd, was a dramatist, and had succeeded me at Smith in teaching drama. At New Haven I had played John Davenport, founder of the city, in a pageant at Center Church on the Green. At Smith I had served on the Community Theater Board. So when the taboos were off, and men were welcomed in plays, it was natural for me to play both in student and faculty productions.

On my retirement the Experimental Theater gave me an album, that ran to appalling size, of the photographic story of my acting.

I think no president ever had a happier time than I in working under Hallie. She dedicated her book to me in phrases quite undeserved, for the obligation was all the other way.

At times she was a stern taskmaster. Never shall I forget the night when at the Act I interval she blasted our acting of Antony and Cleopatra. "It has no life, no spirit! Go back and act, and speed up!" We went back like a football team in the second half. All went swimmingly till the famous purple patch:

"The barge she sat in, like a burnished throne
Burnt on the water . . ."

I declaimed, eagerly gossiping with Maecenas and Agrippa. "How well this is going! How pleased Hallie will be!" and with the thought my memory just went blank. We left Cleopatra out on the Cydnus that night, for Agrippa jumped in without his cue, and all was lost. It was my only lapse.

In the fine frenzy of dramatic composition and performance with Hallie Flanagan, the students took no count of time. After they stopped rolling, they were appalled at the labor to come, of making up unfinished work in other subjects. One year the students put on as their jeu d'esprit an interlude called "The Mystery of the Campus Murders." One after another some of the best students disappear from the college. There is no clue to their flight until someone observes that they are all D.P. students. The classes in dramatic production aid the detectives, and finally close in upon Hallie and her assistant, Lester Lang, using the dead bodies of students who have dropped dead from overwork on her stage as counter-weights for the flies.

"After all, Hallie," says Lester, "it does seem to me that we go rather far at times."

"After all, Lester," says Hallie sternly, "the theater is THE THEATER."

The campus is older, wiser, more intellectual now; it is less spontaneous, joyous, creatively free. Its life is no longer centered in itself. The world, of labor and art, of politics and economics, of international relations, has filled the mind. It is, however, all rather impersonal. The old gaiety is gone, and there is a lot to worry about.

Mingled with all this absorption with life inside college quads ran a strong awakening concern with social conditions outside. Miss Wylie and Miss Buck led it in the Department of English. Miss Salmon in History, and Mr. Mills in Economics brought methods and materials to give it solidity. This poetry and prose had some centers of concern beyond their own gay lives. At times these two interests seemed to oppose each other, as in Grace Healy's blithe protest:

> You smile at all the things I try to write,
> For I know little yet, you say, of life—
> Its blossoming, perhaps, but not its blight;
> Its tenderness, but not its dismal strife.
> I have lived always in a garden place
> With kind, protecting bushes hedged about
> And gently bending trees to shade my face,
> And friendly gates to keep marauders out.
> And through the leafy walls I sometimes see
> Sorrow and pain and hunger just outside,
> Standing so close they almost breathe on me—
> Trembling, I run away from them and hide.
> And they are life, I know, and they are true—
> But, wise old friend, so is my garden, too!

Women's tears were new to me, as weapons of defense. Vassar tears flowed like a river. I sat silent and miserable while student or teacher wept on. The little handkerchief was soon a-drench, and my own big one called into play. I began to keep an extra one in my desk's right-hand drawer, in the wax-candle box where Prexy Taylor had kept the revolver. Soon I stocked up. They became regular equipment for my interviews with students. Knowing nothing of women, I had read that it was good for them to "cry it out." So when it started, I would just pull out the drawer, get a good big handkerchief, and silently hand it to the sufferer. She would say "Oh dear, how ridiculous!" and either begin to laugh or dissolve in new floods. You never could tell. The tears seemed the "reverse Lend-Lease" of their gaiety.

Was it a gag? I used to wonder. I thought the first two or three might have done it on a bet. As the weeks wore on, and the tears did not stop, I began to think it was a fashion some popular heroine had started. Certainly it wasn't Carol Kennicutt, the heroine of "Main Street," about whom everyone was talking. She bowed out of her failure at Sauk Center with the remark that she had failed, but her daughter would not. She was going to go to Vassar, where they ask questions.

This was certainly flattering to Vassar, but I thought Carol would be surprised if she knew how hard they wept at the college of her choice. The system was partly to blame. Everybody seemed to be in a gentle conspiracy to keep every shock away from the tender creatures. It was the fashion to make fun of the "delicate females" of the Eighteen Sixties, but the Nineteen Tens were not much advanced in the essentials of self-control. Whenever a student was destined to receive some painful news, a physician was always hovering just outside my door, ready to hustle her off to the infirmary, for fear she would have a collapse, or "do something." The rest house, Metcalf, soon began to take on the shape of a superior jail.

The communication of painful news, I found, was my prerogative. To cite instances would seem to mock the very genuine sorrow of my hearers. In a group of twelve hundred people, with several thousand in the family groups, disaster or death from disease struck at least once a week. To these must be added the unhappy; the homesick, the lovesick, the merely sick. Discipline was, by order of the trustees, entirely in my hands. I was obvi-

ously so new at this business, so completely unsuited to be a
father confessor at thirty-four, that often a student would begin
to comfort me. "Don't take it so hard," she said. I noticed that
tears came easily with slighter woes. Wounded pride, little fears,
petty entanglements brought them on quickest. The real losses,
the tragedies, seemed to touch a deeper chord below the tear
line.

I noticed, too, as time went on through the years, that the
springs began to dry up. I kept only one handkerchief in my
drawer, and then I gave up the practice altogether. For one thing,
the fear of shock, the dread that a student confronted with a
serious situation would do something in a panic, began to fade,
and then disappeared. Much of it went with the retirement of
our senior physician and our very kindhearted Warden, by which
forbidding name the social dean was known. Most of it died out
with a firmer insistence that the way to greater maturity and self-
control led through trust and confidence that at college students
could "take it."

But the real remedy came with the assumption of responsibility by members of the faculty. The ceremony of leading students to my office for the receipt of sad news became intolerable,
and I abolished it, in gradual steps. I had come to learn that the
mere request for a brief conference was enough to throw a young
woman into a panic. One day I made such a request, and set the
time for the following morning. I was trying to get first-hand
evidence of the complaint from school principals that certain
requirements were too heavy.

"Miss Osborn, what were your most difficult subjects in high
school last year?" I asked.

She told me; I thanked her.

"Is that all?"

"Yes."

"Well, Prexy, *never* do that again to anyone."

"Do what?"

"Send for us without telling why you want us. I didn't sleep

a wink last night. Most of it I walked the floor in agony, won-
dering what I had done, or what had happened at home."

She dried her tears; and for years I followed her injunction,
until the fear of Prexy's official summons wore away, and caused
no more worry than a request to call for laundry at the express
office.

Marjorie solved some of the problems in her own way. Many
a homesick girl felt better after helping her to bathe baby Joy.
A student rushed into the house one day, to tell me that her
roommate had packed a bag and was planning to leave "without
a trace." I sent her back to the room with a note from me, to say
that of course she was free to leave at any time, but if she wanted
to talk it over, I would be at home for the next hour. She came,
pale but resolute to disappear. Her family had forgotten her, and
she would not stand for it. If they didn't need her, she
didn't need them. She agreed, however, to think it over for a
day.

Marjorie, who had discovered that a neglected birthday had
precipitated the crisis, made a birthday cake and took it to her
room. It was all very irregular, not in the prescribed procedure
with young women, but it worked. A good hearty cry, and she
was ready to face her work again. The letter from California
came next day, with birthday messages, and all was well.

We had many similar incidents. Once it was an indignant
freshman who had refused to part with a good-sized black snake
which she had brought with her as a pet. Once a box of pet mice
was the tragedy. One of them was called "Henry Nibble My-
Cracker." Birds and fish were other problems. Girls kept their
pet dogs secretly off campus. All of it was "against the rules."
Some of the rules were abolished, others we tried to explain. We
became so lax that one Founder's Day two girls appeared dressed
as snakecharmers with their pets winding about their necks and
arms. The skies did not fall.

So many pet goldfish were released when college closed for
the summer that Vassar and Sunset Lakes began to teem with

them. Today huge goldfish the size of carp swim in schools, to the great delight of small boys with rod and line.

A student was detected taking nickels from the coin box in the Dutch Oven, a snackbar run by self-help classmates. I was asked to reason with her. She needed the coins at the time to make telephone calls. We talked it over. Her roommate found her on her bed a few minutes later, biting the pillow and beating it with her fists, shouting angrily "Take that, and that!"

Nevertheless we became friends, and one of the most original parties we ever attended was a dinner she gave one night, when she borrowed the Warden's House to work off her surplus energy. Lady Mary, Countess of Winchester, it seemed, had just arrived in America, with her "tame cat," a young poet, her daughter Lady Alice, victim of an unfortunate love affair with a Paris artist, ("I made the trip so she would forget him") and a hoyden younger daughter, whom Lady Mary thought of leaving at Vassar, if she should fancy us.

An English butler in dress suit welcomed us at the door, and a French maid who spoke no English helped the guests to take off their wraps. The meal, a delicious one, was cooked by a tall French chef, and a little 'tweeny helped in the scullery.

"And now, dear Dr. MacCracken," said Lady Mary at a pause in the conversation, "I think it is time for us to hear something about Chaucer."

We lived up to her demands in our imagination as well as we could. The game ended with stunts by the staff in the Warden's parlor. "Just like Barrie's Admirable Crichton" Lady Mary explained.

On a Saturday in spring we joined the Wake Robin Club, and walked to John Burroughs' home at West Park, "Slabsides." The jolly old naturalist took us into the woods, and gave us a lesson in how to see things: arbutus in bloom, birds and insects and the rest of his world. Burroughs, I found, had become a Vassar institution. In his journal he wrote of it affectionately. The college later acquired a superb portrait of "Old John." He told us one day how Walt Whitman came to his room in Washington one night, to ask him what was the most typical American song-bird. Burroughs thought a while, and then proposed the hermit-thrush. For an hour Whitman quizzed him, and then ran off, to write "When lilacs last in the dooryard bloomed," the wonderful threnody on Lincoln's death.

It was characteristic of Vassar's gradual evolution that the ladylike Wake Robin Club should become the Outing Club, with overnight hikes in the Catskills, and long tough tramps all over the county. They wanted a hideout on the farm, miles from the college, where they could "have weekends without taking one," as they explained. So we built them a cabin of logs from trees cut down by the farm men in their spare time. The students called it the "Tabard" in my honor, and we came to share their picnics and "bacon bats." "The Tabard" burned one night, and a more conventional cabin replaced it. By that time the Club had an old Ford station wagon and rambled afar, going off to ski with Dartmouth and Williams men in gay abandon.

It was in these days that rash girls whose conduct I must hastily reprobate went down to the river, tied their clothes to their heads, and naked swam the impure Hudson. They swam the Hellespont, too, just where Leander and Byron did, and told me "it was a cinch." In the '20's they sang:

> Oh, there's the fire bucket,
> And the swimming tank,
> And the bath tub
> That must be clean;
> But sometimes in the spring
> We like to have our fling,
> And so we bone a bike or a machine.
> Then to the creek we trip
> And on the bank we strip,
> Hoping that we won't be seen—
> And who should be swimming in the Hackensack
> But the Warden and the President and the Dean?

World War I hastened the change, but it was inevitable. It was in the air. John Dewey's "democratic" education had much to do with it. Students learned self-reliance by doing self-reliant deeds.

A change of dress, too, had much to do with it. For some years women students had been working in blue jeans while on field trips in zoology, botany, and geology. Scrambling over the rocks or collecting insect eggs in marshes, there was nothing else to wear. On mountain trips to the Rockies, the women found that dude pants wouldn't take it, and changed to cheaper stuff.

With war came farmerettes. Nearly two hundred of them worked at Vassar in 1918. They followed the crops not only on the Vassar farm, but up and down the river. The Vassar gardens run alongside the highway, and the farmerettes blocked traffic as curious motorists stopped to gaze at young women in overalls, weeding onions or picking tomatoes, or handling mechanical potato diggers. At the Eastern States Agricultural Exposition at Springfield, Mass., that September, Vassar farmerettes were the hit of the fair, as their toughened fingers milked prize cows in record time.

Then came courses in play-production, while students had to make and paint their own scenery. Dungarees won the day. Boys' slacks were cheap in the army-navy stores. Soon the big stores stocked them. They didn't fit at first, and the fashion started of rolling up the legs. One stayed up and the other rolled down but who cared? Form followed function, and the new age was on. Men from neighboring colleges might deplore the modern trend, but their women defied their black looks. A Vassar cartoon depicted the end of a beautiful friendship, when a lovestruck youth from Princeton overstayed his welcome, and the bewitching miss of the Saturday prom strolled by in sloppy jeans. "What the —— are you doing here?" says she, and disillusion came.

At a small meeting of graduates in Cincinnati, I ventured the unoriginal observation that brawn, beauty and brains were not incompatible assets. A volcano was touched off. The presses roared with the fierce debate as it was fought from coast to coast.

The Boston father of one student submitted the physical charms of his Phi Beta daughter in support of my claim. A newspaper superimposed them on the torso of the Venus di Milo, who came out distinctly second-best, in the opinion of all fair-minded scanners of the result. Wolves who came to jeer remained to prey. Photos of Vassar girls at work flooded the prints. Some proposals of marriage were most honorably mailed direct to the president's office. One fine specimen from the high Sierras offered to marry any one of the three in the picture that I might select as best adapted to rough outdoor life. "I would myself prefer the one in the middle," wrote the conservative mountaineer, whose own photo displayed him in a Paul Bunyan attitude breasting the mighty Columbia while he hooked a fighting salmon. Conservative graduates shook their heads, but the registration kept its upward climb.

Meanwhile the young women made good in many tasks reserved hitherto for men. Especially in the laboratories they were in great demand, as their brothers went off to the training camps. Once in, they were in to stay. One of the greatest contributions of college women was in the field of nursing, where college women had been in a negligible minority. Vassar organized a "training camp for nurses" in 1918, and over four hundred women just graduated from a hundred colleges put in a strenuous summer, the first acceleration course, as far as I know. In three months they finished more than a year of training. The term ended just as the great "flu" epidemic hit the United States. Into the depleted hospitals went the young nurses, and made a splendid record. Scarcely a single one of the group remained in bedside nursing, such was the demand for them in operating rooms, laboratories, and schools of nursing. Many of them became outstanding leaders in the new profession.

One young woman who saw all this from her sophomore point of vantage was Mildred McAfee, '20, commander of the Waves in World War II. Another, the first Red Cross nurse to be killed in Italy, commanded the Red Cross detachment there. She had a predecessor in Amabel Roberts, the first nurse to die in World War I, who wrote from the field hospital a few days before her death in 1917: "Am I not fortunate?" A tablet in the Chapel keeps her memory, with four other Vassar heroines of the war. On the rise of ground above the Libe, the students planted oak trees in memory of Alvin Treadwell, aviator son of Professor Treadwell and a campus favorite, and other Vassar soldiers.

These generated, I think, the dynamic that did away once and for all with the myth of the fair girl graduate, the "sweet Alice" of the American "Ben Bolt." But in distant cities the myth still lingers. West of the Mississippi young men still talk of the Vassar girl as a country-club product, and professors in many universities still believe that Vassar standards are not serious. The heroines of a large proportion of the movies still go to Vassar. What a thrill went over the audience when in one film Douglas Fairbanks Sr. obtained entrance to the studio of a Greenwich Village lass, and in shutting the door disclosed a Vassar banner pinned across it! In one dance movie Eleanor Powell danced down the six parlors in Main. What could the truth do against fiction?

After all, why bother? The schools knew the truth, because only their best graduates could enter. A quarter of each Vassar class stood No. 1 on their high school graduation list. Many of those rejected made top records elsewhere just to prove how wrong we were. And we were. No wonder the Vassar stereotype was on the "uppity" side.

Some parents, vexed by rejection of their offspring, for years saddened my mail with clippings of their daughters' triumphs elsewhere. I sympathized with them. Had I not been among the rejected myself in a contest for the first Rhodes scholarship? The winner ran off with a barmaid, and the latest word from him was that he was a barker on a London sightseeing bus. But even that did not entirely salve my self-esteem.

The fact was, that while our first hundred were without question entitled to entrance in the competition, the rest were a gambler's chance. We knew too little about them. There were too many variable factors. Probably a hundred rejected candidates were fully equal to their successful rivals in every way.

By President Coolidge's day, the women's colleges were labelled radical. Mr. Coolidge himself gave currency to this myth. The fact was, of course, that they were centers of conservatism. But Mr. Coolidge gravely cited the Vassar wisecrack:

"How do you feel this morning, optimistic or pessimistic?"

"Neither, just antagonistic."

The women's colleges in self-defense fought back, and thus increased their bonds of cooperation.

Yet it cannot be denied that there have been black sheep. Two Vassar women were listed as spies for hostile countries. One in Paris was sentenced with her husband for spying against the French Republic. One, a Hungarian, was accused of forming huge cells while she was on a tour of the United States. She escaped, but some of her victims did not. There have been a few communists known to me. Once, while watching a Communist parade in New York, an old lady stepped out of line, and still carrying her glowing transparency with its Communist slogan, cried: "Here I am, Dr. MacCracken, take a good look at your Vassar women."

She, at least, had graduated in the good old days, I consoled myself.

A magazine article by one of my first students complained that Vassar was "unreal," that it unfitted students for the rough actualities of life. From its gentle ways to the rough and tumble of American social and political life came a shock too severe to withstand. Some retreated into themselves, others became cynical and dissipated, others lived in a pleasure world protected by husbands with money. Thus you could choose either Coolidge's "hotbed" theory or the "cloistered dreamland" of my college writer. Both were true, and both were false.

So far as I ever learned anything about college women in

thirty-two years, I tried not to generalize. Each of the ones I came to know—and I stayed on campus most of my time—were individuals, unique in temperament, in mental equipment, in physical vigor, and in case-history. History never repeated itself with them. I handed diplomas to nearly ten thousand, and knew something of the two thousand who did not stay to get them. No two ever even looked alike, except the identical twins. You could make up statistics about them, but they didn't tell you anything you wanted to know. Nothing but the personal relation gave you that. I lived and worked in a maze of guesswork about them, but I never fooled myself into thinking that I really knew anything measurably true about them as a group.

Beginning with this notion of diversities I came to believe that any uniform plan of education for them was folly. The one thing I could reasonably be justified in expecting with any show of uniformity was a certain quality of response. As college students with exceptional opportunities they might be expected to do their best. If they did not, most of the time, Vassar was no place for them.

Not all the time. We had to take account of obstructions. There was mental fatigue, emotional instability, and, most difficult of all to remedy, the failure of the college itself to provide a worthy program, stimulating and satisfying.

At first I was slow to understand that the business of a college is to discover unity in all this diversity. In twenty years of study and teaching, I had not learned that all these students, infinite in their variety and complexity, owed one and the same allegiance to their nation or their community. Of religion I was to some extent aware. It meant much to me, and I had had a religious experience during my three years as teacher in a Protestant missionary college. But by consent my college was secular. It could speak out for religion—but not too far. Our students were Protestants for the most part, but also Jews and Roman Catholics. Some were members of no church. Beyond this diversity I could not penetrate.

Patriotism was a different matter. American life, though imperfect, seemed pretty good to me, after spending five years of my thirty-four in other countries. I saw it endangered, not so much from without as from within, not so much from the weakness of its political structure as from the wrong kind of education. Democracy demands responsibility on the part of every citizen. Our education was too authoritarian. It gave lip service to the ideals of responsibility, but did not teach them. Even when they were taught in the classroom they were not practised in the college life.

It was therefore my hope that in the practice of equality on campus, the students might not only come to believe profoundly in it, but to develop those traits of self-reliance, tolerance, mutual aid, and above all, justice and fair play in their relations. This could be done, it seemed to me, first by developing a system of student government, with all powers transferred to the students that they could maintain efficiently; and second, by developing a political association among them, which would serve as a forum for the study of current questions.

I had seen something of student life at Oxford and elsewhere, and I knew how great a part the political system played in it. I did not want that system in an American college, because our students were not ready for it, but chiefly because a student is a student, not a partisan. The more partisanship, the less reflection. European students were made the spearheads of every political drive. The prisons were full of them. That, it seemed, was the destruction of scholarship, though of course in a world crisis, students must do their part. But study, too, is national service, or isn't it?

Vassar had had a worthy history in the development of student government. Back in Matthew Vassar's day the students had won the faculty's somewhat reluctant consent to elect their own representatives for conference with the faculty. President Raymond attended the first meeting, and as he fully expected to be elected their presiding officer, was somewhat rudely set back when the students voted that he should be asked to leave the room.

It was twenty years, however, before the students won any real power, and then it extended only to the extra-curriculum, and to that part of it restricted to student relations on campus. It was my hope that we might transfer to student officers full control of social life, a large share of academic discipline, and a genuine share, at least in the formative stages, of the development of the curriculum and of all college policy.

A young Bryn Mawr graduate walked in upon a tea-time group of students one day. They were discussing the hows and whys of college government with Marjorie and me.

"But what are you students here for?" she asked. "Your job is to oppose the president, not to learn from him."

An article of mine later published in *The Yale Review* outlined "The Growth toward Democracy in American College Government." It was considered very radical at the time, and effectually closed the door to any activity of mine in the higher levels of university administration and politics. Nevertheless the students of Vassar came to believe in it, and to practise it. On the whole, trustees and faculty did their best to play their own new part in the plan.

Instead of an honor system for the elimination of cheating, the curse of American colleges, it was affirmed that in adult society every citizen will wish to see the laws enforced, provided that he have a hand in making those laws, and that the law is enforced by his peers. We therefore transferred to the students all authority over their own membership that could legally be transferred.

Since the contract of education is with the parent and the college as a corporation, severance of the contract could legally be made only by the president. However, in only one instance can I recall refusing to enforce a suspension or expulsion, the case being one of a hasty and ill formed suspicion, requiring a Supreme Court decision to modify. For the rest, progress toward complete control of social rules by the students went steadily forward, and management of examinations, library use, and other college services was assumed by them.

The faculty already had appointed a joint committee of faculty and students. I well recall its early meetings, in an atmosphere of frank and unrestrained hostility. Time passed, and the joint committee came to consider every important college question before it came to a vote in any body. The joint committee had no authority of any kind, even to instruct its own members. Each group reported its deliberations as they deemed best. But the conference was of great value in preventing action without fair notice. The faculty went further than this. They agreed to adopt no measure affecting student life and work without previous conference. Thus in those days students voted on proposed changes in the curriculum before they were voted on by the faculty. No harm ever resulted.

The trustees, in their turn, established a committee on Undergraduate Life, and discussed the general college policy quite frankly with them. It was after one of these sessions that Russell Leffingwell, formerly Assistant Secretary of the United States Treasury, and an active trustee, expressed himself as so delighted with the students' maturity in dealing with these questions that he wanted to signalize the day in some way. Thus was built the openair classroom, with its praise (by Pericles, of course) of free discussion, and of the value of action after it. "For we Athenians have the peculiar power of thinking before we act, and of acting too."

Of the relations of students with the staff of employees, not so much can be said. While there has been no prohibition of such relations in any way, the workers themselves have preferred not to play the game with the students as fully as have professors and trustees. There is, however, a good understanding. The employees shared many student privileges. They played golf, used the gymnasium and Students Building when hours were convenient. The pavilion in the golf-links was built as a token of appreciation by employees for this policy. The respect of employees for students' political interest grew after the passage of the nineteenth amendment, and many of them joined the new Political Association as it took its place with Self-Government, Church, Dramatics, and Athletics, as the fifth major organization on campus.

Other enterprises were later successfully started by students. The Hoot'n'Owl, a snack bar, started in Main as a candy kitchen, became a successful after-show tavern, competing with off-campus in spite of temperance rules. The Cooperative Bookshop, under the genius of Marion Bacon, has been outstanding among college enterprises the country over. The total budget of student enterprises rose to well over a hundred thousand dollars annually.

Student self-government most benefits its own officers. They are given a really wonderful training. The infusion of an understanding of the whole process and the indoctrination of every student with the spirit of responsible citizenship rest, as they do in civic life, upon the leaders to develop. During those early days it was hard work. I had had no experience of the democratic process. It was hard not to use the despotic powers conferred on me by the trustees. Doubtless at times I did use them, but, I hope, unintentionally. I tried hard to keep hands off, both my own and those of others, while the students worked painfully at their problems. Out of my work with these students have come the most lasting friendships. From the process emerged an estimate of the American college student as a serious, mature, and thoughtful person, well able to manage her own student affairs.

There are delinquents in every society. Vassar, I found, was no exception. Against college rules the chief delinquency was going AWOL, as in other communities where discipline comes first. One night, seeing a truant trying to climb in a dormitory first floor window, I helped her in with a friendly "boost." She pitched headfirst into the dark room, and then reappeared to thank her unknown aid. Her face was a study. The story was told and like all such tales, became attached to so many college heads that I wonder now if it really did happen to *me*.

French leave almost cost Edna St. Vincent Millay her diploma. After the faculty had asked her indefinite suspension for unauthorized absence, I was in a quandary. By trustee vote I had the power of veto in faculty action, but had resolved never to use it. In this one instance I did so, but only after a stupid delay, which kept Vincent from her own Class Day and Baccalaureate. For the latter she had composed both words and music of a hymn which she called "St. Vincent." Her diploma, however, was duly presented to her at Commencement in defiance of faculty opinion. I was ashamed not to have acted earlier, for there were few students who had done more for their college than this young poet. She forgave us, I think, for she wrote her charming "The Lamp and the Bell" for the 50th anniversary of the alumnae in 1920.

An elaborate system of cuts and absences from college was maintained, most of the wardens being engaged in records throughout the day. Their value was slight, for any clever girl could outwit them. More personnel guidance by wardens would have made the endless bookkeeping superfluous, and better morale would have resulted. Next to cutting, and far more serious, was cheating. It was a rare offense, and visited with immediate expulsion. I protested violently, and succeeded in getting the rule revised. After all, I claimed after a visit of Tom Osborne at the college, we couldn't allow the sister college at Sing Sing to have more advanced views on penology than we did. So each case was studied. We soon found that emotional problems were back of all our cheating, but it was several years before we thought of psychiatry as the best though not the only answer. Our first reference to psychiatry was in 1923, when a student came to my home at Christmas time, telling me of her dread of return to her parents. We took her in, explaining to the father by telephone and asking him to leave her in our hands for a few days. Dr. Slocum of Beacon helped us, and convinced me that a consulting psychiatrist was needed on our staff. Dr. Austin Fox Riggs was his suggestion, and for years was of the greatest aid. It was to be twenty-five years, however, before adequate provision was made in our budget for this indispensable service. Suicide by a member of the faculty was followed by two student suicides just before Dr. Riggs' appointment. After his appointment no student suicide occurred at college, but several occurred at students' homes. In each case the illness had been diagnosed at college, and care and treatment urged.

The college health department was in mortal fear of suicide, and ostrichlike tried to prevent it by secrecy and by a hovering watchfulness that bordered on the police function at times. Hysteria, a product of emotional disorder, was severely dealt with. The education of physicians at the time included little training in the field of mental illness, and the unknown was dreaded. However, we were fortunate to escape in our utter ignorance. Members of the faculty as well as students suffered from mental disorder. Elementary knowledge on our part would, I think, have prevented the losses that we suffered, for in later years several attempts were frustrated, and treatment proved successful. The old belief that one attempt made any cure hopeless has been replaced with a more courageous view. We carried a number of risky cases successfully to graduation by removing the patients from disciplinary methods of dealing with their problems. Dean Thompson was of great value in all this.

Intoxication was unheard of until the days of prohibition, and was rare throughout. A few sharp disciplines, and a close cooperation with local sheriffs and judges made the temptation less inviting, but for a time conditions were fairly serious. Again, however, it was recognized that the offence was a social one.

I have said that psychiatry, valuable as it is, is not the only answer. As religion is often judged by the private lives and personal temperaments of its ministers and priests, so psychiatry is judged, and sometimes unfavorably, by the personal conduct and morals of psychiatrists. The fact that there are several schools of psychiatry gives a basis that generalization in this field is not yet possible.

I recall an afternoon at the home of Comtesse d'Haussonville in Geneva, where I met my first Freudian. He was a Swiss. In a most offensive way he began to cry down all other approaches to human problems.

In our early work with psychiatrists we found that they were apt to forget the burden on other students of keeping up friendly relations with an emotionally disturbed roommate. We could not agree to some of their solutions of such cases, because, we contended, Vassar was not a mental hospital.

For a time it looked to some folks as if psychiatry would replace morals and even religion as a resource in time of trouble. No longer should we say "His truth shall be thy shield and buckler." Then we began to notice that many of the techniques of the mental hygienist were those of religion. A local minister in Poughkeepsie wrote a book: "Mental Hygiene as Practised by Jesus." There was truth in it.

Already in one college at least the dean is a psychiatrist. One distinguished psychiatrist came into my office one day, and made the cool proposition that he should take over the entire responsibility for college personnel,—my job, in other words.

"You have men in your boiler-house who should be professors, and professors who should be bricklayers," said he. "You know nothing about personality."

His own ego was so inflated that I began to wonder whether he had escaped from a neighboring institution. It was with the greatest difficulty that I could get him to realize my own wish to keep on with my job in ignorance of his techniques.

Personnel experts, similarly, offered to do the dean's work of counseling students. Open conflicts often ensued. Today there is recognition that our knowledge of human personality has been vastly extended by our study of normal and abnormal psychology, but that we really know more about those things through folk life than we thought we did. Religion, philosophy, and plain human kindness and common sense have not been displaced; on the contrary they have been confirmed. In the matter of guidance, an important phase of college work, I should put character and personality of the counselor as the first requisite.

There is about some psychiatrists an air of superiority that is almost insufferable. Curiously enough, they are also inclined to be quarrelsome, and to say the most extraordinary things about one another. Sometimes they incline to be cryptic, as if their profession was a hieratic mystery.

Fortunately, Vassar, in Dr. Riggs, found a man of religious background, and his associates were imbued with his ideas. We came to believe that all teachers should have a knowledge of the elementary principles of psychiatry, and some acquaintance with its techniques. The psychological aspect of religion and morals, we learned, was profoundly important. With some relief, however, we came to think that psychiatry was an aid, but not a substitute, for education.

Our first professor of Child Study, Professor Smiley Blanton, students told me, said to his class: "In order to understand childred, you must first understand yourselves. The work of the first semester will therefore be psychoanalysis."

I am not sure that the students quoted him accurately, but I think his approach was not misrepresented. He was a Freud student and a great friend of the eminent founder of the art. At the present time, he is cooperating with a minister, Dr. Norman Peale, in conducting a clinic at a church in New York City.

Every teacher should be equipped to counsel healthy, normal young people, and should know enough about abnormal psychology to know when to send for the psychiatrist. But how many of us are abnormal? I don't know, but hospital beds for mental patients outnumber beds for all other patients in this crazy country. Charles Doughty, author of "Wanderings in Arabia," says that in fifteen years he never saw an insane person in that uncivilized sub-continent. Maybe they were all killed. Maybe the new education, with the aid of psychiatry, will reduce our own numbers. At present there are enough mental patients in New York State hospitals to populate two cities the size of Poughkeepsie.

I learned a great deal from Dr. Riggs and his successors, and came to depend on the psychiatrist as an indispensable member of the college staff. Marjorie served for years at the Hudson River State Hospital as a member of its Board of Visitors, and got a sense of the fine work carried on there. My criticism refers only to a few of the psychiatrists I have worked with in the early days, who were followers of the school of "Dr. Knock." He, as everyone knows who has seen Romains' famous play, put everyone in the village to bed.

"Pour les médecins?"

"Non. Pour la médecine."

While on the subject of psychiatry, I will inject a word about homosexuality. As principal of a Syrian high school in Beirut in 1903, I had learned a good deal about the Levant and about boys. Of girls' crushes and women's affairs I know nothing. Certainly I learned nothing at Vassar. It was in the scope of our physicians and psychiatrists, and there I left it. I have the impressions that what we consider aberrations from the norm are the result of inner compulsions, and are not to any great extent the result of immediate surroundings. Statistically speaking, I should guess that there is little difference between coeducation and separate education in such matters; between those who go to college and those who do not; between one sex and the other. But I do not know.

Theft was our besetting vice, I learned. It usually began with careless and unconscionable "borrowing" of other students' clothes.

> Jane had a pair of Bunkerman books
> And Jane had a brand new Ferguson hat.
> Jane had a room-mate
> Going up to Yale Prom,
> "And that," said Jane, "is that."

We did not take it so gaily. A definite campaign was started to engender a better morale. When a student was caught shoplifting in New York, and when local shops reported serious losses, the drive was understood, and student government cooperated vigorously. Here, again, our aid came rather from psychiatry than from college rules and discipline.

These incidents, and others affecting alumnae that came to the president's desk, showed simply that the group was human. On the whole its social record was apparently above average. Wild rumors spread like epidemics round Poughkeepsie at times. At one time it was said that the State Hospital was filled with victims of college education. Investigation brought the number down to one case, but the rumors ran their course.

Carelessness with fire was chronic. A well-drilled fire department, with good equipment, and heavy fines for offenders, accompanied the educational campaign. Our one serious fire started in a chimney in the maids' wing, however; and our barn buildings burned more often than students' homes. A record of over 80 years without the loss of a college building or faculty dwelling has been maintained.

On one occasion I noticed the considerable embarrassment of a professor at a personal interview in my office. Finally his courage was mustered, and I learned of the extensive holes in my pants which had escaped my attention while dressing. Stray shots from fire-extinguishers at a fire in a professor's dwelling the day before had done the damage.

Professor Macurdy, walking beneath windows of Main, was once completely extinguished by a flaming steel wastebasket thrown out by an uneducated student. She had been waxing her skis. The wax caught fire, was flung in the basket, and the paper blazed up. She threw it out of the window. Fortunately, Miss Macurdy's abundant gray hair and good sized hat took the damage. When I asked our classicist what she thought at the time, she said: "I just said to myself, the revolution has come. Be calm. Sophrosunë!" Classical training has its merits.

HISTORICAL EVIDENCE.

A song of the 'Twenties.

When we heard from Dr. T
Of our ancient pedigree
Traced back to the Cambrian sea,
Much impressed were we,
Though they say man and baboon
Are but a minute in a long afternoon.
How in the world do you know that?
She told us so.

As we grow older
This earth gets colder,
Which used to smoulder—
But as householder,
Our philosophy of life
Will make us each a perfect wife.
How in the world do you know that?
She told us so.

Let us pause in admiration
Of the racial obligation,
And amoeba's propagation
Of his generation.
'Twas an epoch-making spasm
Rent in twain his protoplasm.
How in the world do you know that?
She told us so.

As he grew older
The sea grew colder
Making him strong ter
Linger no longer.

He developed respiration,
Then maternal abnegation,
Hence the present generation.
She told us so.

etc.—16 stanzas, added year by year, as succeeding freshmen classes completed the course in hygiene taught by our redoubtable professor of physiology, Elizabeth B. Thelberg.

ENGINEERING VASSAR

WHEN VASSAR OPENED in September, 1865, a young farmer and his bride joined the curious public. The college needed more help on its farm, and Albert Flagler was engaged. For fifty years he and his wife lived in the old Dutch cottage on the rise of ground above the Vassar pond. Albert ran the mill at first, where the flour was ground. Then he took over the grain corn, and finally the fine herd of Holsteins. The college bought more land until its 750 acres were as good a piece of farming as old York State could show. The Cornell experts that came down to advise us said so, anyhow.

Flagler and his right-hand man, Frank Dedrick, were type specimens of the American farmer. When things got hot or tight for me at college, I would wander down to the barns, and profit by their philosophical conversation. They were so much wiser than I was. They were humble, too, although they were the real aristocrats of the Hudson, coming from old Valley stock. To Albert Flagler Vassar College was "the Family," whom he loved.

"Ease em along, Doc, ease em along. Don't drive em hard. You can push things a little, but not far. 'Tain't worth the difference."

I learned from him what little I ever knew of strategy in campaigns for faculty approval of my programs. Propose it straight out, as clear as could be, in the fall, and then let the seed grow, cultivating a little and keeping the weeds down by going over the ground once in a while. Then in the winter months, when weather keeps folks discontentedly indoors, encourage the leaders to bring the matter up, and push for a vote after full debate. Nothing after Easter. Let the ground have rest.

We had a wonderful teacher of piano, Miss Kate Chittenden, who lived in New York, where she maintained a studio successfully for over fifty years. She kept a room at Mr. and Mrs. Flagler's, and in the evening after dinner in Main, she would light her old farm lantern, and take the way that led across the road to spend a quiet hour with them in the old parlor.

"After the city roar, and the girls' chatter, it is just like a benediction to be with the Flaglers," she told me. "They are *good* folks."

Frank Dedrick was younger. He and his wife, who was by official appointment historian of the "town" of Poughkeepsie, lived down at the fork of roads, in another old Dutch cottage. Frank, now retired, was modern. He studied at Cornell. His herds and flocks were inoculated, his milk pasteurized. His fields came to know the tractor. The twenty horses dwindled to a team. He gave up cutting the ice on Vassar pond, after the college bacteriologist, Miss Benton, showed him bacteria living in the ice eight months after cutting and storing. Besides, the ice-house burned down.

Frank's daughter Helen is an alumna, a bacteriologist in her own right, with a record of service at Rockefeller Institute. The college for many years had the custom of educating daughters of its staff, both in trades and in professions, without charge. So many daughters were born in Faculty Row, that it seemed as if the hormones knew all about the generous plan. I recall one year the daughter of a janitor standing at the head of her class. And why not?

To an unexpected degree I found Vassar a self-reliant college. Three miles out in the country, with no stores worthy the name near by, Vassar was not in the city limits, but in what was at first called Bull's Head, after the tavern on the corner of Raymond and Main. The tavern down the road from the old Vassar farm in English Norfolk, where I once had a tankard of ale with quiet neighbors who talked of Vassars still about the village, was also the Bull's Head. Stubborn folk.

But "Bull's Head" was beautified into "Arlington," and was little sweeter for the name. The rickety trolley line, with bouncing and swaying cars that went off the track too often, did not encourage trips to town.

Vassar, thus turned upon itself, became almost independent of the community. Supplies were bought wholesale out of town, coal by the carload from Clearwater, over to Poughkeepsie to the Vassar pocket and thence by Vassar wagons; meat and fish from New York, and all else if possible. The college harvested its own ice, drank its own milk, produced its own eggs, fowls, and pork, and most of its vegetables. One-third at least of its food cost was right from its own farm. For years the college had made its own gas, and paved its walks with the tar. Some years before I knew Vassar an electric plant had been installed, on direct current, and the comptroller was paying off its debt to itself at the rate of seventy-five thousand a year, while every other account was starved to make this one good.

Vassar baked its own bread in Jewett basement, whence, as the students told me, it was piped to the other college dining rooms, with other pipes for ice cream. The asparagus, they were equally sure, was endowed; for the college garden in spring served it three times a day in season. Spinach, and later broccoli, were similarly "endowed," along with "fish-eye," a sickly tapioca that looked languidly up at homesick girls along toward Christmas time. When Main dining-room burned at supper time on February 12, 1918, the fish-eye bade them a sad farewell. It froze and stayed all winter.

Water came from shallow wells scattered all over campus, but chiefly from a deep well behind Faculty Row. Not for years was any change thought of, until the college geologist, Professor Hills, urged that the broken nature of the subsurface allowed of contamination. Then the college gave up, and hitched on to the city supply, to drink pure Hudson.

The sewage from this village college of nearly two thousand souls was "scientifically" disposed in a drainage farm area. The plan was suggested by a trustee, Professor Ellen Richards, teacher of sanitation at Massachusetts Institute of Technology. This famous alumna was the founder of Home Economics, and the coiner of the word "euthenics," the art of controlling environmental conditions. She had a great influence in her time. I have heard that America gave up the privy at her behest. Certainly you find Ellen Richards Houses at State Universities and technical colleges, where modern houseplanning is taught.

With responsibility put on me for all these services of police, fire prevention, water, gas, electricity, steam heat, sewage, food production, and use as well as for ordinary maintenance, we had carpenters, plumbers, roofers, painters, plasterers, steamfitters and other heads; I felt like the mayor of a little community. Nor was it long before I learned that the system would bear inspection.

It began, as usual, with the students. Some of them came to me indignant over what they saw of the life of the three hundred maids employed by the college. Knowing nothing whatever of hygiene, economics, or labor problems, I dodged. The students were told to be patient, and Marjorie was asked to make quiet visits to the housekeeper. She found maids sleeping in rooms without windows, in the hall where the bread was baked. Other things were of the kind. I took it to the trustees, without effect at first. But when Mrs. Minnie Cummock Blodgett, of '84, was persuaded by me to come on the Board, a Committee on Household Management was set up to replace the gentle amenities, and things began to happen.

Stokers shoveled coal into our roaring furnaces for fourteen hours a day. We burned fourteen thousand tons a year of good expensive anthracite. Then one day, crossing the grass, I noticed a wisp of steam rising from a crack in the frozen ground. The steam pipes were laid in shallow troughs, and water leaked in. As winter wore on, we seemed to be boiling the whole water level.

The students called the Quad the "Valley of Ten Thousand Smokes."

I found the college had no plan of its underground lines. It was all in the head of George Law, the superintendent of the heating plant. He was a desperate man, trying to work a system that had got out of hand. His harassed face did not invite inquiry, and when I sought him out he burst out in angry invective at the impossible job. The steam continued to rise for three years.

It was the same story all over the place. We had a large force of excellent workmen, but little money provided for materials. The services were starved. Later, when I came to visit other colleges I found the like conditions. Colleges might be places of learning; they were certainly centers of monumental inefficiency. Over it all was a "hush-hush" policy of silence stemming usually from some wasteful member of a board of trustees, who was running the college business to suit himself. I didn't like it, but what could I do? I had been told that my job was education, and that the all-powerful executive committee of the Board was responsible for the business side. So, in gross ignorance, I let things slide, until the whole thing blew up three years later, and I found myself held to blame, and, no doubt, justly.

The "staff," as our workers in trades and occupations were called, were a wonderful lot of people. There were over four hundred of them in all, including the three hundred maids. Over the women presided Miss Blanche Barrett, an immensely stout lady of most delicate manners, whose tiny feet could not carry her far. She was a person of great authority, and to tradespeople and, in fact, all outside circles she was the head of the college. Marjorie reported that in New York stores she was told that the president of Vassar had just bought a corset.

As the college had no place for storage of supplies, we lived from week to week, and almost from day to day. Emergency stocks of pipes and other metal goods lay in piles scattered about the back yard. The losses were large. A supply valued at $1500.00 was dug up by our watchman in the yard of one of the neighbors, who proved to be an employee. But such doings were rare. The staff as a group were loyal and honest. Miss Barrett posted the menus twice a week, and the general superintendent tried to fill the orders. One night a couple of mischievous students substituted a menu of their own choosing, a really magnificent table d'hote, almost worthy of Delmonico's. Poor Superintendent Gillespie tried desperately to fill the order, but there was not enough steak in town. He did the best he could, however, and the students rejoiced in a meal beyond their dreams of plenty. Emboldened by success, the mischievous pair, G. Folks and A. Taylor, tried it again. Miss Barrett had posted scouts, and they were caught. I prevented their expulsion.

The janitors, who dwelt in basement rooms no better than slums, were a grand lot. With the janitor of Main I often played checkers, and found him an expert. As an undergraduate at N. Y. U. I had thought myself a good draughtsman, but I never won a game from old John.

Alfred, in another "dorm," was something of a disciplinarian. "Miss Smith, the girls are pretty noisy tonight."

"I know, Alfred, but they have self-government, you know, I can't do anything."

"Well," he said, "we'll try what I can do." He went upstairs, and in a minute dead silence reigned.

The students, wrought up over conditions of labor at Vassar, and stirred by what they had learned in courses under Professor Mills, had built and endowed the Good Fellowship Clubhouse, a social center where classes were taught the illiterate ones and recreation provided under a trained social worker. Miss Barrett did not permit the social worker to enter any other building than the Clubhouse.

Later a student who died abroad in war service bequeathed five thousand dollars for the benefit of Vassar maids. Thus began the Ruth Cutler Fund, which has expanded into a welfare fund of much benefit.

Miss Barrett was an intelligent woman, and if she had had

the means would have done much to improve living conditions. But she saw no way out of her problem. She was unhappy and friendless. The same heavy hand of absentee control imposed upon her a separation from faculty life, and she had no resources within herself.

She took to candy. Every week she ate a five-pound box of candy. The end was certain. The physicians warned her to stop, but she could not or would not, and she died of a surfeit. Yet she was loved by the maids, who once struck to defend her government, and won a victory for her.

To be a maid at Vassar was a step up the social ladder in Dutchess County. The maids were admirably trained. Many of them were daughters of farmers and farm laborers, who learned housekeeping well. They were in great demand as housewives, and the turnover of employment was terrific. Maids took students as models of dress and deportment, and were everywhere taken to be Vassar girls. Some of Poughkeepsie's best families were replenished from this source, and new ones started. We knew many of them well. On "Town Sunday" we often gathered a group of them in our car, and took them down to their churches as we found them waiting for the trolley.

Occasionally a promising maid would be given a scholarship by the Students Association, and would start up the ladder of learning. One of Vassar's faculty today once ran the mangle in the college laundry. Another former maid is a leader in Poughkeepsie society.

Fortunate were the hall maids. Women of long service and steady habits were entrusted with the care of college buildings. Barbara of the Library, Ida of the Chapel, Mary Ryan of Sanders Chemistry were some of many who ranked with the faculty in college life. Faculty and students alike loved them. Gradually they became members of the faculty. Mary Ryan knew every piece of glass in chemistry, and when she left, three persons had to be employed in her stead.

"Mary, where is that retort with the double curved neck?"
"Oh, don't you remember, Miss Mary? You broke that three
years ago, when you stumbled."

When we installed retirement and pensions at 65, Ida was
indignant.

"Why am I discharged, Mrs. MacCracken? Did anyone ever
find a speck of dust on the pews, dark chapel and all? What's
the complaint? Who did this to me?"

The Library in Barbara's day was a place of utter silence.
Barbara did her cleaning with a skill so high no sound ever came
as she plied her mop.

Enter one day Bubs Johnson, Professor Burges Johnson's
youngest, with her terrier Rags. The moving mop excited the dog,
and he attacked it. Barbara pulled to get the mop from him,
Bubs pulled Rags, and in a moment the whole Library staff,
alerted by the growls and cries, were at one end or another of
the tug of war. Finally Rags was pulled off and Barbara went
down with mop and overturned pail. She never got over her
disgrace.

A young carpenter, recently bereaved, fainted one day on a
ladder. He was assigned to the grounds as a night watchman.
Thus began the career of Jack Hennessy, whose name will stand
high among the roll of honor of employees who have helped to
create college tradition. Jack is a poet, or minstrel, whose ballads
were sung on the force. When Ray Wigg went through the ice
in Vassar pond while clearing it for student skaters, it was Jack
who pulled him out and made a song of it. When my second-
hand car was surreptitiously repossessed by an angry dealer it was
Jack who sang delightfully "As I Sat in My Low Priced Car." Is
a bicycle lost? Ask Jack. Campus thieves and other miscreants
were caught by him. When an alumna was raped on Sunset Hill
by a farmhand of retarded mentality, it was Jack who made the
arrest. Possessor of innumerable confidences, he never betrayed
anyone. His cheerful face has been a guaranty of security for

thirty years. One of his colleagues who kept the college gate, believe it or not, was Charley Lockit, a worthy successor to Vassar's original Cerberus, Mr. Gatehouse.

It was natural that the early trustees, who knew more about business than education, should have bequeathed their meeting rooms to the comptroller and his staff. Vassar's comptroller was George W. Polk in 1915 ("There is nothing so deaf as an Adder"). The little sign at the cashier's window daunted timid freshmen, who were frequently scared away for days from paying their bills, while Mr. Polk wrote down his columns of figures in beautiful copperplate.

"Doctor, we'll wind up the year with a surplus of thirty thousand dollars."

"Hallelujah!"

"Doctor, I made just a leetle mistake yesterday. It won't be a surplus, but a deficit; and its thirty-five thousand, not thirty."

"The President has a sick headache. He can't see anybody today."

Thin as a toothpick, and keen as a Yankee, George Polk was a figure out of Dickens. He looked as if he had been designed by Cruickshank.

His father was an English sailor who jumped ship at New Orleans, and hid in the canebrakes by the river for days while the bloodhounds were baying. He starved and rode the rails till he came to Poughkeepsie, where he worked in the shipyard, rising to be a shipbuilder of no little repute. Poughkeepsie ships in those days carried Fortyniners round Cape Horn. Polk had many a good story to tell, and I used to sit in his workship at his house on College Avenue where he whittled at beautiful ship models, and revel in his artistry in wood and word. My son Calvin has a beautiful ship model of Mr. Polk's giving.

Louis Gillespie was a bird of another feather. Formerly a buyer for the Hudson River State Hospital for mental diseases, he never got it out of his head that students and faculty were any other than inmates of a correctional institution. Maybe he was right, at that; but I spent a lot of time diverting from his bald head the wrath of one or another enraged inmate.

Gillespie was a swivel-chair expert. He sat in it all day, even through the lunch hour, when a glass of milk and a cracker seemed unaccountable for his more than comfortable bulk. How many employees we had I think he never knew. He added one here, another there, until the time of retrenchment came in the first pre-war recession, and with a broken heart he resigned, to die soon after. He was more sinned against than sinning, I think, for he had no budget to guide him. He never knew what the Executive Committee would do next, or what trustee or faculty would descend upon him with authority to order an improvement. Most of his time went, as was the custom, in passing the time of day with drummers who sought his patronage.

Lou Gillespie's right-hand man was Alonzo Sagar, our superintendent of buildings, an intense, nervous person of Lincolnian stature, who in these days of personnel guidance might have been sifted out and made a professor of philosophy. Our conferences started with building problems, but usually came round to questions of immortality and the nothingness of matter. Sagar was a religious leader up Kingston way, and was sought after as a speaker. His educational ideas would have pleased old Matt, for he saw to it that his sons learned every technique of women's work, cooking and sewing, washing and ironing, and all the rest. Whether he believed in complete equality for both sexes, or whether he wanted to set his sons free from the monstrous regimen of women, I never knew. His life at Vassar made him a bit misogynic.

But he was a skillful builder, and the college owes him Williams House and Alumnae House, erected without contract. He was much troubled when a bolt of lightning struck Williams just at its completion, flattening one chimney and shaking the plaster loose from the ceiling as if an earthquake had rattled it about. It was some consolation to him that lightning struck other buildings, but he thought my insistence on rodding the Library and the Students Building quite supererogatory.

Gathered round Sagar was a squad of jolly Scots, with Rob Cameron at their head, skilled artisans in every craft. They welcomed a Mac, and soon I spoke on Burns's birthday, and sang his songbook through, exhilarated by patriotism and a wee doich an' doris.

Once later on a Founder's Day, we sang them all again, dressed in full regalia, kilts and sporrans and plaidies and a'. Man, hae you ever wound yersel' in a thirty foot tartan, or tossed yer bonnets up at the "Relief of Lucknow"? Hae ye never seen it? There's a play for ye. If yer heart doesna' beat the faster when the foe is at the gate, and the skirl of the bagpipes comes to ye, soft at first but louder and louder until the pipes burst in the door, and everybody's shouting "Scots wha hae," then ye're no true Scot.

"How came you to make the hazards so cannily?" I asked Wully Chrystal on the golf course one day.

"Because, d' ye see, ah was born on the links at St. Andra's," was the reply.

The buildings of Vassar were sadly run down. All of the available funds were being used to pay off the debt on the electrical plant and the wiring of the halls. Dr. Taylor had been a "great builder," as his memorial tablet testifies; but it was not a time of good, sound construction, for all too much of it had to be done over again in the quadrangle halls that were erected in the days of Vassar's poverty.

Two architects were rivals for his favor. Allen and Collens were first on the ground with Strong House in 1892, planned to start a new series of buildings en échelon, either side of Main. But York and Sawyer won the competition for Rockefeller Hall, and persuaded Dr. Taylor to alter his plan in favor of the quad.

Ed York and Phil Sawyer were table-mates at draughting boards, in the office of McKim, Mead, & White. Phil's sister, I was told, wrote her brother that Prexy Taylor was very responsive to bright colors. Upon this hint they acted, their garish perspective of a classroom building winning the award. Rockefeller Hall became the first of the many successful designs of this famous firm. Swift Infirmary and New England Building, one colonial, the other Beaux Arts, were soon added to their laurels.

But Collens had Strong House to his credit, and the quad pattern secured the other houses for him, while Mrs. Frederick Thompson chose him to design the Library. Taylor, Josselyn, Cushing, Skinner and Kenyon Halls were later trophies of Collens, and Van Ingen too, while York won Blodgett, Kendrick, and the Warden's House. This last was my first responsibility, for Mr. and Mrs. Pratt asked me to choose the site for it. We spent a long afternoon tramping the grounds. Mr. Pratt inclined toward a spot between Jewett and Students', but Miss Palmer and I thought it needed a garden. So we chose the place near the observatory, although we were told no one would ever go so far to call on Miss Jean Palmer.

She was Ed York's cousin, as it happened. For her York designed a perfect gem of English cottage style, the best building on campus, to my taste. When its lovely garden was set out, with the hemlock hedge for privacy, I bought some additional hemlock plants to hedge a Shakespeare Garden down under the great white oak by the Fonteyn Kill. It has become a favorite spot for campus weddings, as well as for Shakespeare scenes acted by classes in English. Its path led to a beautiful weeping willow, grown from a cutting brought by an alumna from the grave-site of Napoleon at St. Helena.

The division of architects is partly responsible for the variety of Vassar styles. But the givers of Alumnae House chose Joseph H. Hunt for their design, and this choice determined the style of Williams House nearby. Dr. Sanders had chosen his nephew to design his two laboratories. The two ladies who gave the chapel selected Coolidge, while Students went by the wish of the anonymous giver to William Mitchell Kendall, a nephew of

Vassar's Maria Mitchell. Personal choices like these made uniformity impossible. Perhaps a stronger president could have brought about the dominance of English Gothic, as Collens urged during his term as consulting architect. I was not in love with the style, however, though I did suggest French Gothic for Skinner as a way to William Skinner's heart and purse, since his sister Belle Skinner loved France so well. It was, I think, the deciding factor in his choice of Vassar for this memorial building.

North Hall, renamed Jewett House by alumnae petition in 1915, was built by the trustees during Dr. Taylor's absence in Italy, from designs by the professor of art, Dr. Lewis Pilcher. It seems to have been built for defense against embattled students, its balconies and crenellated roofs affording every opportunity for a prolonged siege. Mr. Pilcher later became State Architect, perhaps because his style was suited to armories.

French Renaissance, English and French Gothic, north and south colonial and modern (Baldwin, 1940), English timberwork of pepper and salt—could any group be more incongruous?

I'm afraid I haven't helped much to bring about a harmony. But it does not look as bad as it sounds. Most of the buildings are well placed and the vistas do not introduce strongly clashing features. Main, Blodgett, Skinner, and the Library invite comparison with no other halls.

Then there are the trees, the merciful, forgiving trees, giving glimpses instead of great masses of masonry. Vines, too, do what they can to soften the harsh clashes of the styles.

"Why didn't you sod the damned thing?" said a donor one day at Princeton, when he came back to view his costly gift. "Plant it out," has been the Vassar motto. I began it in my first year, when the silver maples of the quad were set out. They are glorious in spring and fall. Complaints about Jewett have ceased since their stately branches have taken it under their protection, and the firs on either side prevent the side views.

Here are some of the crimes we did not commit during those years. A marble arch at the end of Coolidge Avenue. A dining

hall for the whole college in the middle of the quad. A big build-
ing in the Floral Circle. Another in the Shakespeare Garden. A
Psychology Laboratory just north of Main. A library west of
Rocky. Greatest of all, the completion of the Pilcher design for
Jewett with wings to east, west, and north.

Next to old Main, which is easily the best design on campus,
the modern Baldwin House appeals to me, and the interior
architecture of the art library in Van Ingen Hall. They do their
job with great economy and simplicity. If I had it all to do again,
I should strive for these things.

There is, of course, a case to be made for variety. The Vassar
campus is a record of the changing fitfulness of the times, when
no style predominated. The stately plan of Jefferson inspired
Students, as Oxford towers inspired the library and Taylor. Oxford and Cambridge today, it may be added, have not preserved
their unity. But a total plan for the future, it may be hoped, will
help to bring all this era of fits and starts into some order at last.

Nearly every day Marjorie and I formed the habit of walking
after lunch for an hour together. To these walks is due the choice
of sites for most of Vassar's later buildings. We found we could
walk twenty-eight hundred feet in ten minutes, if we were brisk
about it. No building is more distant than this from any other.
But I forgot the dawdling after class, and other business of the
interval. Result, a bicycle college, in spite of signs ironically an-
nouncing that pedestrians have right of way. The life is healthy
for the quick, anyway.

Over on Swift's Hill, something over two miles from the college gate, an old road ran south to the cider mill. Juniors always
took their little sisters, the freshmen, for doughnuts and a glass
of cider to Kimlin's mill. They sat by hundreds along the old
stone wall, singing college songs, and drinking the heart's blood
of good Dutchess County apples. Then home again in gay groups,
in the soft autumn glow, under the scarlet and gold of the
maples.

Ralph Kimlin, owner of the mill, was and is my good friend.

An Englishman, he pastured sheep, and built a pond to wash them in. He started a museum, too, adding much from Vassar's surplus of fossils and arrowheads and stone mills. The mill has entertained Vassar folks for three generations. Van Ingen, the first art professor, painted it, and Clarence Brodeur painted it again in later years.

Kimlin's grandmother was a Fetherstonehaugh from old Ireland. Once in 1930, Marjorie and I were picnicking by the roadside near Athlone. We were under a cypress tree for shade, and used an old tombstone as our table. We found it was a Fetherstonehaugh of the eighteenth century, no doubt being kin of Mr. Kimlin. The local pronunciation we found, was Fanshaw.

Ralph Kimlin started a guest book, which soon held many a worthy name, for Kimlin's cider is deservedly famed. At his request I started it off with a posy.

"At Trumpyngton, not ferre fro Cantebrigge,
Ther goth a brook, and over that a brigge,
Upon the whiche brigge ther stant a melle,
And this is verray sothe that I the telle."
Still goes the brook, and still the Kasper Kill
Winds its slow way below the cider mill
Where Vassar girls, perched on the wayside wall,
Make merry like the clerks of Soler Hall,
With doughnuts, hot dogs, cider, and with fun
Less rowdy than the Scots' at Trumpington.
But Vassar "bumps" old Cambridge, 'tis confessed;
Kimlin's pure cider's of the very best,
And though we make no special brag of *morum*,
We're just a mite more careful of decorum.

"Mr. chairman," Mr. Dimock would say, "as we do not seem to have much business on hand, I would like to return to my customary theme of the grounds. We must provide for the future. I do not want Vassar to appear grasping. It is merely my thought that our permanent policy should be for her to own any contiguous property."

The trustees laughed at the theory of contiguous property, but iteration is a strong persuader. Vassar already owned over six hundred acres, which went popularly for a thousand. Matthew Vassar's two hundred had been tripled by adding the Davis and Hospital farms, the latter purchased from Vassar Hospital.

Now we added the Pheil farm of a hundred and ten acres, which we named for our beloved farmer, Albert Flagler. The Worrall farm of fifty-four, and the Wing farm of a hundred and twenty acres, were added in 1924. The Hughes farm of fifteen was secured to provide for possible storage and unloading facilities by the railroad track to the north. It might be profitable some day to sell our coal pocket in Pokey as factory site. We had even the wild dream of burning oil and piping it to the furnaces from the new siding.

With the addition of dwelling lots on College and Fulton Avenues, and of a lot on Manchester Road, our expansionist energy was spent. What a lovely ground it is! Sunrise Hill was now ours on the western slopes, from which little Matt had first viewed the college. Below it lies Sunset Hill, with its great pines and spreading pinetum. The golf course runs to and fro between. To right and left rise Downer woods, great groves of tall oaks, and an acreage of pines, planted twenty-six years ago (1924), at the urgent plea of Franklin Delano Roosevelt, our trustee from 1923 to 1933. His term included his period of recuperation, his governorship, and the early weeks of his first term as President of the United States. He accepted designation as honorary trustee thereafter. As a tree-farmer, as he called himself, Mr. Roosevelt enjoyed our campus of specimen trees, but he wanted the students to have a practical demonstration of reforestation, and the pine woods on Sunrise were the result.

Vassar's first pines, on the path from Taylor Hall to Main Building, were planted by old Matt himself. "Come here and help me, young lady," he called one morning to Miss Barbara

Grant, the youngest member of the first faculty, as she passed up the walk. So she did, and held the young trees upright while the old man pushed the soil round the young roots of what are now the great pines and spruces. Fifty years later, she told me this.

A thousand species, Mr. Downer tells me, fill the campus and the 1875 Arboretum, as the two brook slopes have been named. Mr. and Mrs. Paul Zehe (Emma Chamberlain, '75) are the patron saints of our trees. She appreciated our early efforts to save trees which had been starved for lack of nourishment, and the Zehe bequest of nearly half a million dollars was the result. The small sum spent was certainly bread on the waters. Mr. Zehe's will binds the trustees to spend a thousand a year on the trees hereafter. Trees and flowers, and green lawns, are the best of teachers.

Vassar grounds are full of stories. There is Crooked Quad, for instance. The legend runs that Matthew Vassar, Jr. staked out with his own hands the site of Vassar Brothers Laboratory, Vassar's first addition, in '78, after the original Main, Calisthenium and Observatory. Matt, Jr., thought he had made the new site in line with Main, but his eye betrayed him. Overnight the superintendent put the stakes parallel, but the angry trustee next morning detected the shift, and set them back askew. Vassar Brothers Laboratory is gone, the building being not worth the cost of restoration, according to the engineer's report. But the damage was done, New England Building was laid out on the crooked axis, and first Sanders Chemistry, then Sanders Physics, followed suit.

Mrs. Sanders, for whom my good friend Henry M. Sanders named his first gift, was one of the leading workers for woman suffrage. She was one of the New York group to propose a vote for suffrage in the '90's. It was defeated overwhelmingly. The group, headed by Dr. Mary Jacoby, returned crestfallen to the city, and decided that they knew nothing of practical politics. The result was the founding of the League for Political Education, of which Mrs. Sanders became the president. The League founded Town Hall, and the famous America's Town Meeting of the Air is an offshoot of Town Hall, and of the pioneer work of Eleanor Sanders.

The Physics Laboratory, bequeathed by Dr. Sanders in his will of 1920, is guarded by "Benjy," an old pewter statue of Franklin the printer, which for nearly a hundred years adorned the entrance of Harper Brothers, the great publishing house in Franklin Square. When Pierpont Morgan came to the help of Harpers, Burges Johnson, our Professor of English, secured it as a gift, and it stood in his office during his term.

Class trees rise all over campus. The first class, 1867, planted ivy on Main. The next two classes planted the great swamp oak and beautiful "weeping" elm that stand guardian at Main's front door. Every class since has either planted or adopted a tree, with ceremonies more or less informal. The tree ceremonies in the nineteen years of which I chiefly write were charming interludes, beautifully rehearsed. One of them, an Irish folk tale, required a goosegirl and a flock of geese, which the producer concealed for a week in the basement of Students. I can see her now, as she wandered across the lawn, while we waited breathlessly to see which tree she would choose, to rest and sing beside.

When the Chinese gingko south of Main was chosen, a Chinese classmate sat beneath the tree in the moonlight, singing to the strain of a moon guitar, while her whole class, kimono-clad, sang with her. The sentiments of such moments may bring a smile, but the Art of College is a creative experience. It should never be lost. From the point of view of a college president, it brings more returns in firm loyalty than does the Science of College. One is learned, the other is lived.

Unique on college grounds is the Floral Circle, whose great hedge of arborvitae, from the first year, kept Paul Pry from seeing what he shouldn't. Originally planned as an arena for outdoor exercises its border was soon exploited by the Professor of Physiology and Hygiene, Dr. Avery, to give more natural exercise in the planting and care of flowerbeds. Every student had a lot, and cared for it. The old setting-up drills are a thing of the past in physical education, but the love of gardens persists, and again the Art of College supplanted its technique. Conservation became a hobby of early graduates. One of them, Helen Clark Putnam, who taught physical education in the '70's, gave Vassar her Conservation Fund of nearly a half-million, to teach conservation in after years. So the flower circle bore its fruit, as the trees have borne theirs.

Near the Floral Circle is the Venus de Vassar, a tree stump oddly resembling the torso of an antique goddess. Topiaria, however, has not been followed with the trees. They are in a fairly natural plantation: evergreens near the arborvitae hedge, maple trees in the Quad, poplars by the brookside, pines on Sunset and oaks by Vassar Lake. The rest fit in wherever they can. Great specimen trees on the lawn are the admiration of visitors. The superb white oak that overlooks the Shakespeare Garden is, I think, the tree from which a survey of 1798, now in the Adriance Library at Poughkeepsie, begins its measurement.

Vassar grounds are under the care of an English horticulturist, a man of Kew Gardens, who is a scholar in the world of botany. Many graduates have kept up their friendship with Henry Downer, and exchange seeds and seedlings. They have read his columns in New York newspapers more diligently than they do the learned quarterlies in their major fields, I am sure.

Sometimes the gardener becomes a tyrant. When we built a conservatory on the roof of our garage, the gardeners appropriated it for their own. When we started a few flowers for a personal flowerbed, Marjorie was soon forbidden to pick her own flowers. It is no wonder that the goldfish bowl in which we swam brought us wry smiles. How unkempt is our present home at Hornyback, how primitive, how utterly satisfying since we have become our own gardeners!

Yet it is good to have healthy and well-pruned trees and lawns. A mother once said to me: "All I needed was just to walk around Vassar grounds, in order to make my choice. Any college that is so kind to its trees is sure to be kind to my daughter."

From May to October, Vassar is a place of beauty. Its early flowers in Shakespeare Garden, its thousands of tulips, its hundred species of lilacs, its rhododendron and laurel, the fragrant vines in summer, and all its other pleasures, must give some sense of beauty to the most worldly soul. Our foreign students have remembered Vassar for beauty more even than for enlightenment, as their letters show.

One can forgive all shortcomings, and bid "farewell, my boke and my devocioun" when one breath from the apple trees blows into a Main window.

> Vassar in beauty dwelling
>   Through all the changing year,
> Hail to thee, mighty mother,
>   Lovely, serene, austere!
> Praise we thy blooming springtime,
>   Rose-red thy June we praise,
> Crimson and gold thy autumns,
>   Crystal thy winter days.
> Vassar enthroned in beauty,
>   Glad at thy gates we throng,
> Mother of all our dreaming,
>   Lift we to thee our song.

Is there any lovelier tribute to any college than this Vassar song by a Radcliffe graduate, the late Grace Macurdy of our Department of Greek?

During the late war, wishing to learn more about Shakespeare gardens, I wrote to the head gardener at Birmingham, England, which has the most famous garden of this kind. The letter and the literature which I received by his kind attention, proved that even in the terrible blitz England was true to her gardens. I doubt whether any other single factor has had so much influence in character building as the English love of gardens. It is a part of the English heritage I would not willingly let slip.

WE HAVE WITH US TONIGHT

IT WAS A WARM SPRING SUNDAY. The perspiring young preacher was on his mettle, for it was his first invitation to a college pulpit. The students were trying hard to listen. Suddenly a whiff of wind blew all the preacher's manuscript off the pulpit and down among the pews. There came a gasp of sympathy in the dead silence. The young man paled, then pulled himself together and went on. Dr. Spear's reputation was made, and he had no further cause to complain of inattention.

Dr. Timothy Stone was pounding away one day. Suddenly he jumped as if a snake had bit him. He looked at the fleshy part of his right palm, and pulled out a thumb tack, up to the head embedded. The blood spurted, but he pulled out a handkerchief and finished his sermon without further gesticulation. He kept the thumb tack as a souvenir of the way they torture speakers at Vassar.

"Follow me, and I will make you fishers of men," a preacher once announced as his text, and wondered why the students laughed. The next Sunday another preacher read the same chapter, but carefully omitted the laughter-rousing verse. The effect was more disturbing than if he had read it.

Little episodes like these whiled away some of the hundreds of hours which convention seemed to think I should spend as chairman at lectures, or minister-in-charge at service. A few of the lectures were interesting enough in themselves to hold attention. More often the lecturer's quiddities kept me amused. Still more often I put on an expression of rapt attention and held it motion-

124

less throughout the lecture, while my thought busied itself with next day's plans.

Most lecturers mercifully limited themselves to fifty minutes. A few were urged on by their audience. Vilhjalmur Stefansson was kept talking for three hours while no one left the room. John Cowper Powys insisted on talking long past suppertime, and would not desist when I asked him. I got around in front of him and waved my arms until he stopped, while the students shouted. Powys would not speak to me afterwards, and I don't blame him.

Some of the English lecturers were just plain rude or thoughtless, some were eccentric, some were very bad showmen. They mouthed their sentences, dropped their voices to the inaudible point, and even talked to the blackboard or the screen as if no audience were there. Some of them, like Beerbohm Tree or Alfred Zimmern, condescended to tell young women how they should behave, as if they knew. Women affected some lecturers oddly. Malinowski, the anthropologist began: "Vassarines, Vassarians, Vassaronians—how shall I call you, Ah, I have it: Vassarettes!" He was drowned in laughter, which went on and on. The unmentionables had been mentioned. Malinowski tried to quiet them by saying: "Well, it may be funny, but it can't be as funny as that." They laughed the more. This particular bit of anthropology was not in his field.

Emile Hovelaque, Inspector General of Public Instruction in France, declined to proceed until a glass of water had been brought. It was brought, but Hovelaque tasted it, and finding no sugar, waited till I went out and brought the lump, then insisted upon a spoon to stir it. By this time his audience had escaped him. He had been asked as a member of the French High Commission, to talk of the role of French women in the war. He told us solemnly, that it was the duty of women to think. That was all.

Another member of a French mission came to give a Red Cross talk, on care of the wounded in the war. We did our best for him. A drive through the best part of Poughkeepsie, a stop for tea at Cliffdale, Miss Kenyon's estate with its gorgeous view, and a walk through the Circle with its tulips and lilacs, and girls at archery, enchanted him. As we walked toward chapel, we met the one girl in college who spoke perfect French. Now he was bewitched.

The introduction was made, and Monsieur was off in the most poetic French. "Never have I seen so beautiful a city as Poughkeepsie. Such exquisite vistas, such avenues of charm! The great mountains! the mighty river! and the young ladies of Vassar, in their bower of lovely fragrance," etc., etc. Fifteen minutes of it, and I was obliged to interrupt him and release his spellbound audience. Not one word of Red Cross care for the wounded.

I had some difficulty in getting lecturers to the lecture. William Howard Taft was to lecture in Students, and tried to get into my automobile, but stuck halfway. I pushed and pulled, but it was no use, he couldn't make it. So we pulled him out with difficulty, and walked. Neither he nor I spoke a word *en route*.

A. K. Taylor, Food Director under Hoover for a starving world, had no audience. We sat and sat, but none came. The students were just not interested in the world that lacked food. Finally Dr. Taylor accepted his luck and departed, not too well pleased to be thus bottled up. I was so mortified that the whole college felt sorry for me, and turned out *en masse* to hear St. John Ervine. They sat and sat, and no lecturer came. He had decided not to come, because it was snowing in New York, and he dreaded the drifts, poor man.

Tagore bargained with me like a rug seller, coming down by steps from eight hundred to two hundred dollars. I would not sign. It was, I like to think, his agent who signed his name to the telegrams, but the bargaining smacked of the Oriental bazaar.

William Butler Yeats, at Smith, had got off the wrong side of the train, and wandered about town for two hours, while I, as chairman of lectures that day, searched frantically for him. Finally, exhausted, I went back to the station to see if his baggage had been checked, as a clue. There sat Yeats in a complete abstraction, eyes open but unseeing, huddled against the stove at the end of the bench.

Sometimes a lecture exhilarates a lecturer to the point where he thinks more highly of himself than he ought to think. A great art historian mistook Josselyn House for Alumnae House after his lecture, and, after a vain ring of the doorbell tried to climb in by the window of a student bedroom, to be caught and led off campus by one of our watchmen. He had insisted that he knew his way, but the shrieks of the disturbed girls betrayed him.

Vachell Lindsay was so exalted by the success of his reading of "The Congo" and other poems that he serenaded the seniors afterwards, as they hung perilously from the corridor windows of Main. He made up his own cheer for Vassar, borrowing an apothegm from Josh Billings, whom he was delighted to find as local hero. He chanted:

> Better not to know so many things
> Than to know so much that ain't so!
> Vassar! Vassar! Vassar!

It took hours to get him to bed, for he was intoxicated with a far more heady wine than mere alcohol.

Sometimes lecturers got into trouble at our house. "Mac-Cracken!" shouted G. L. Kittredge, "I can't turn the water off."

I rushed out. The guest room floor was six inches deep in water, a cataract was pouring down into the hall, and the unclad scholar seemed about to be washed away. Lowering my head, as I always do in crises, I rushed to the basement and turned off all the water. My wife, Marjorie, always composed in crises, waded in and turned off the faucets.

Kittredge recovered his composure. "I hope this will not be

told of me. I was never considered especially adept in the manipulation of mechanical contrivances," he said at breakfast, as the water dropped from the ceiling on the pantry floor.

But what a wonderful lecture it had been! "Shakespeare's Villains." How he revelled in it, and what an ovation the old professor received, and how he loved it!

Other guests were less delightful. Solomon Reinach, resplendent in uniform, was obviously impressed with his new military rank. Though in private life he was curator of the Luxembourg Gallery, and had never smelled powder, he shouted about the house as if it were an army barracks: "Ricci! Ricci!" while his aide responded from the toilet, "Oui, oui, mon Colonel, je viens."

Some lecturers were not just lecturers, during these war days, or later. They were, to put it diplomatically, "correspondents" of their governments, gathering news about the United States and its aims. S. K. Ratcliffe, one of the best extension lecturers in Britain, learned more than he spoke, and other Englishmen emulated him.

At a meeting at Vassar, John Erskine and Burges Johnson debated some subject.

"But don't you see," said Burges in rebuttal, "everything you've said is really what I've contended. You're really in full agreement with my argument."

"In that case," said the imperturbable Erskine, "I take back everything I have said, and affirm the opposite."

Our most popular lecturer in the early days was Samuel McChord Crothers, clergyman and essayist, who charmed his audience with his really artistic reading of his quiet humor. Another was Canon Hannay, better known as G. F. Birmingham, noted for his Irish stories. For him and his wife I laid out an itinerary, which they faithfully followed. On their return I asked Mrs. Hannay, "Now that you've seen everything, Grand Canyon, Yellowstone, and the rest, what has impressed you most about America?"

She answered me according to my folly.

"I think it is the whistling peanut stands in New York. It is such a quaint use to make of the steam."

At its best lecturing is an art, a minor art of the theater. At its worst, it is a racket.

Count Keyserling behaved like a charlatan, and lectured like a mountebank. Granville Barker, like the fine actor he was, said nothing in particular, and said it so well that he captivated a crowded Students audience. Later in our kitchen he drank two full quarts of milk, to make up for the dinner he had foregone. "Never eat before a performance," he said. Alexander Meiklejohn in younger days was a showman of the first order. Quizzed afterwards by the faculty, he seemed only an Artful Dodger in the debate.

On the whole, I felt relieved, as the officer in charge, that Matthew Vassar's endowment for lectures was no larger. But Vassar women became gluttonous for lectures. In my early days, they were given in the old Main chapel, and our Warden, Miss Palmer, would rout out enough seniors to make a showing that was scarcely more than decent. In later years lectures were often adjourned to larger halls because the eager throng could not be accommodated.

"You could get a liberal education by just going to outside lectures, Prexy," one of them complained to me. "Why do you bother with a faculty?"

Times for lectures multiplied, until the calendar showed half a dozen in a single week. But the lectures of entertainment dwindled, as the faculty scorned the offerings of lecture bureaus, and invited lecturers whose subjects were akin to the courses of study and enlarged the students' range of vision. This, I came to think, was their true mission in college.

We had our moments at the concerts too. Once, at a symphony in Students', a slight earthquake set the chandeliers swaying. The students rose in alarm.

"Sit down," roared the Professor of Speech, Miss Cochran, and the panic was allayed.

At another concert, this time of the Cleveland Symphony, the leader, Mr. Sokoloff, turned to bow his acknowledgment of the generous applause. Catching sight of some students ensconced on the sill of a second-story window on the side of the gallery, he was alarmed at the risk and said he could not play further because of it. Miss Palmer then stood up and waved to the girls to get down. Instead they disappeared out of the window. The whole orchestra rose in consternation, thinking the students had killed themselves. They accepted with reluctance Miss Palmer's explanation that there was a roof of the wing just below the windows. It was some time before their shattered nerves permitted them to go on with the concert.

Student housekeeping in Students Building was not too strict. When Harold Bauer gave a piano recital, the pedal stuck on the floor. Mr. Bauer leaned down, removed the wad of chewing gum from the pedal, and walked off. It took the apologies of the whole Music Department to get the unnerved artist to return.

My worst agony in early days was the steam pipes. They clanked and rattled so fiercely that they made readings impossible. Usually, in my capacity as assistant janitor, I had all pipes shut off, no matter how cold it might be, twenty minutes before each lecture, but sometimes I forgot this precaution, and as a result spent the time of lecture in some basement, wandering about and closing valves, while bemoaning the lot that had made me the valet to visiting lions. No one enjoyed my services more than an alumna poet-lecturer, who loved the irony that placed me at her regal service, while she waited, in queenly dignity. Times had changed since she had wept in my office over some infringement of our rules.

POKEYTOWN

A PART OF THE BUSINESS of a college is to
learn as well as to teach. Like Chaucer's clerk of Oxenford, it
must be always at both tasks. To learn its community is obviously among the first of collegiate duties. Yet such was the
dominance of books that students and teachers alike went
through their towns with blinders on. Out of this ignorance grew
prejudice, and out of prejudice came active hostilities. The old
cry "Town and Gown" still echoes, though there are no more
pitched battles in Oxford. When I studied there as a John
Harvard Fellow, I saw students armed with rocks concealed in
towels go down the High Street, breaking every shop window as
they ran.

I found in Cambridge and in New Haven active and even
dangerous hostility to the university and all it stood for. Tax
exemption, low wages, bad living conditions for employees, antagonism to city projects, but most of all the superior attitude
and intolerable bad manners of the university group were resented. The intellectuals set themselves apart as an upper class,
siding with the well-to-do in all civic affairs. University ladies,
Marjorie was told at Yale, did not call on anyone who lived east
of Orange Street or west of Prospect. It was fatal to encourage
acquaintance beyond these respectable bounds.

My instincts rebelled against all this. In Cambridge during
my three years I joined a local church, and became an active
member. I was asked to direct its Riverside Mission, in a district where the people were either Italian or Negro. They were

131

an underprivileged and even lawless group. We helped them to some chance of recreation. It was good to play with them.

At New Haven the Italian Davenport Mission took a lot of my time. Naturally, then, when we came to Poughkeepsie Marjorie and I thought of ourselves first of all as people of Poughkeepsie, whose first job was to study the town and learn about it.

The townsmen gave a dinner in my honor. It was held in the Pompeiian room at the Windsor Hotel. I was a shy, rather tense young man, and when the good-natured guests rose to greet me as I stood up to speak, it seemed to my timid glance that the room was vastly greater than I had thought. People were rising on every hand, as far as I could see. "Great Scott, what a crowd! Can I reach them all with my weak voice?"

Raising my vocal organs to four jackass-power, I bellowed "LADIES AND GENTLEMEN."

"Pipe down, my young friend," said Mayor Wilbur at my side. "Them's mirrors."

The flood waters in the valley of humiliation poured over me. I never knew what I said after that. With infinite courtesy the Poughkeepsians heard my feeble remarks to the bitter end. That particular nightmare stayed with me for long.

But I got over it, as young folks do, and worked hard on my public appearances in the river town. I found it a tolerant, incurious place, preserving much of the placid Dutch temperament with which it had begun. Its name, I learned from Miss Helen Reynolds, our really distinguished and learned antiquary, was Uppuh-ke-ipis-ing, the "water place of reeds," where in old days Indian runners had rested on their errands, transphrased by the Dutch into Rust-Plaets, Sleeping Place. Sleepy it was, and not interested in growth. It was never in any sense a college town, like Northampton. The Chamber of Commerce seemed more interested in keeping new business out than in furthering its entrance. Its people were conservative to the last degree. I learned that when some Democratic schoolmaster had tried to get the Legislature to take the "t" out of its misspelled Dutchess County, the farmers went Republican, put back the "t" where it had been, and stayed Republican thereafter. By the merest accident Franklin Roosevelt ran for the State Senate in the one year when Republican mismanagement of policies caused an overturn, and was swept into the office from which he spring-boarded into the office of Assistant Secretary of the Navy. It never gave him a majority in all his four terms as President, although he brought fame and visitors to the prosperous county.

Il Progreso, the local Italian society, asked me to speak on Columbus Day at their banquet. Their toastmaster, Tony Tesone, was a good tailor, and very good friend. His English, later much better, was then rudimentary. His introduction became historic.

"Ladies and gents: tonight we like hear somet'ing 'bout Christoforo Colombo, not just Poughkeep! I ask ever'bod' who is can tell us somet'ing 'bout Christoforo. Nobody know an't'ing. Nobod' in all Poughkeep know a dam t'ing. Den my frien', policeman Mansolillo, 'e tell me Tony I got a frien' in New York, Magistrate Freschi. 'e know a lot. Maybe 'e come to our dinner.

"So I write a nice letters, and I say, "Pleez, Magistrat' Freschi, you come-a Poughkeep' talk about Christoforo Colombo? I get a letter next day: 'Yes, Tony, I come.' 'e bello! ever't'ing fine. We all set.

"Den, few days after, is come anoda lett'ra. Magistrat' is sick, no can come. Mio Dio! What to do? I ask ever'bod' again— nobod' know one dam t'ing 'bout Colombo. Nobod' will speak.

"At las', yesterday Dottore Furlone tell-a me: 'Tony, ees a young fella' MacCracken is just come presidente at Vassa' College-a; 'e like to make-a speech alla time, mebbe he make a speech for Christoforo Colombo!'

"So, I ask-a heem. He tell-a me 'Sure, I come.'

"Ladies and gent: I introduce."

In 1918, Tony entered the K. of C. service, and became famous at St. Nazaire as the fellow with the coffee for men just off the ships.

I came to know Poughkeepsie pretty well. It was the center of one curious trade, that in wild animals. A German broker supplied most of the zoos with their stock, it appeared, from a Poughkeepsie side street.

The famous Smith Brothers Cough Drops were Poughkeepsie's proudest boast, and the Smiths were the chief benefactors. Y.M.C.A. and Y.W.C.A. were the gifts of the first "W. W." S. who was in the first year of Vassar the steward of Main Building. His account book, containing odd-looking menus and copies of letters complaining of conditions, was given to our library. Young Will had to cook vegetables for four hundred without an iron kettle, apparently. A continuous war was waged between him and Cyrus Swan, Matthew Vassar's secretary, who had been made superintendent of the college. Smith could not stand it, and left at the end of the year, to become Poughkeepsie's wealthiest citizen. His statue adorns the summit of a city park.

Marjorie was asked for advice by a student group who wanted a social outlet in the neglected second ward of the town. The result was the founding of Lincoln Center, one of Poughkeepsie's best-known institutions. It occupies two buildings and good-sized recreation grounds. The newer building is named the Marjorie Dodd MacCracken Gymnasium. Built during the depression by a bold scheme of Marjorie's, suggested to her by Tom Corby of the lighting company, it was so named by the Common Council at a surprise party for Marjorie. I don't wonder they admired her high finance. The Center, which she served so long as president, is out of debt, I should add.

Our first touch with Arlington was the Visiting Nurse Committee, which came as a result of health reports. The death of our little boy in New Haven had made us very sensitive to the need of preventive medicine. When, shortly after, Joe Weber came along with a proposal to organize a county health association, I agreed to help, and served for eight years as its president. Mrs. James Roosevelt was vice-president, and we met at her home. This was my introduction to her son Franklin, who became interested in our polio clinics.

Pursuing the plan of integration with the town, we gave a reception to the good folks of town and county.

"And when did you come to our county?" asked a patronizing trustee of an old farmer who attended.

"In 1680, Madam. My name is Knickerbocker." And it really was. We discovered to our great delight, that the skilled artisans and small contractors of the neighborhood were an extraordinary group of workers. Without exception in the thirty-five years we have known them, they have been of the highest character and exceptional skill, and the kindest of neighbors.

In town was a circle of good fellows who called themselves the Indians—convivial to a degree. They loved a "party," as they called their open air picnics and clambakes. Their chef was Judge Morschauser of the State Supreme Court. I was told he had worked for a time as a butcher. Certainly he loved to put on a butcher's apron, and to broil steaks that French restaurants never saw or equaled. Another Judge, George Spratt, was second chef. Later a mayor of the town, he was tuneful, and started off the round of ballads for which the Indians were famous. His great piece was the elephant song from "Wang." Frank Lown, president of the Savings Bank, a delightful companion; thin as a wisp and delicate of frame, sang lustily of the "oak and the ash and the bonny willow tree."

> "When I was a young lass in Rosemary Lane
> I earned the affection of master and dame,
> Till along came a sailor boy, fresh from the sea,
> And that was the beginning of my sad miseree."

Each man had his song. I chose as mine a Hindu love song which I had learned from Carl Waugh, son of a missionary, and a Harvard student.

Up na kooi na hin hai jee.
Dhan jo ban ka ghurrub na kee jee,
Sar par maut na ma na.
Ek din nisa ho ga bunda,
Tu du beh bin pa ne.
Sada na bagh na bulbol bolen
Sada na bagh behara.
Sa na rai yan husn jawana
Sada na suhabat ja ran . . .

Many years later, acting in Mrs. Flanagan's production as the King in Svapnavasavadattha, a Hindu fourth century play, I sang this song to our Hindu musicians. They rocked with laughter, and asked if I knew what it meant. I did not learn.

Peter Troy, banker and broker, is one of the best known figures in Poughkeepsie life. Friend of most members of the "River Families," he had been active in nearly every town movement. The rowing regatta owed everything to his friendly aid. The house planning work owed a like debt. With his friendly guidance I started the Vassar Bank, to relieve the college from acting as banker to all its students. It grew in twenty years to assets of over three million and is now a branch of the largest bank on the River, the First National, and has its own new building. Its stock doubled in value during the period, although in the depression it had secured a loan of $45,000.00 to maintain capital structure. The loan was soon repaid.

Peter Troy's office had a basement, which he fitted up for a drop-in luncheon. Over the fireplace he wanted a motto, and Horace's line was drawn upon at my suggestion, suitable for a fun-loving broker:

"Carpe diem, quam minimum credite postero."

The town and the county came through the "next day" very well. No bank in the county went under in 1933, and the farmers stuck it out on the farms till better times came.

With a Dutch and later a strong German element in its population it was natural that music should become Poughkeepsie's favorite art. Singing clubs were its chief social recreation. Its most famous citizen, however, was an artist, Timothy Cole, the engraver on wood, who through the publication of his wood-cuts and comments on art in the Century Magazine did much to interest Americans in the history of painting. We became devoted friends of the Coles, and still cherish copies of his work that he gave us with a too generous hand. Knowing of his needs I suggested to him that he should make an engraving of the Library at my expense. This he made by copying a painting of the Library by his son Alpheus. From the sale of copies I was able to create the Timothy Cole Art Fund.

Timothy Cole was an Englishman, a character straight out of Dickens. When the Coles were in Florence Timothy suddenly decided that the costume of fifteenth century Italy was your only wear. He dressed his whole family, children and all, in the best Medicean mode and sallied forth, only to be arrested for attracting crowds. He was a very small man, and his wife was tiny. The artist could not bear to have her pattering about the attic over his head, and so Timothy designed a house with eaves so low that even his wife could not stand up in the attic. So—she went anyhow, and crawled about on hands and knees.

In her health campaign Marjorie had a hard time persuading farmers to adopt measures of health. "I don't believe in opening windows at night. It starts drafts. I tried it once, and couldn't see it made the slightest difference in my health."

Among her neighbors visited were Mr. and Mrs. Vess and their daughter, Miss Effie Vess. This reminds me that the English Department once had an applicant in English Speech training, named Hullah Bellew. Believe it or not, I saw the letter.

The Hinkley family owned the trolley line, and their summer cottage on Winnesook Lake was visited, with climbs up Slide and Spruce mountains to pass the time. Rhoda Hinkley claimed credit for suggesting "Happy Days" as the Roosevelt campaign tunes. It was sure-fire.

Their trolley went off the wire for the last time in a glorious ending of the line, when the buses came. A most jolly party of the Indians made the last trip together, and blew the emergency whistle so hard that by the time Taylor Gate was reached the brakes were useless. The old trolley car kept right on past the gate and down the road, just missing a dive in the lake by miraculous fortune. But the Indians' luck was with them, and no one was injured. This was known as the "Last Sigh of the Trolley" in the town lore.

A merry, friendly town, with no pride of origin or old family, with no one but Josh Billings to claim as famous citizen, and living by his philosophy of live and let live—a town with many ethnic groups living peaceably together, and with good records in Red Cross and other services, only one murder in thirty years, no great destructive fire, no scandals of wide note—happy is the town that has no history. I was not sorry I had cast in my lot with it.

The field work of the students in the town was opposed strongly by Professor Mills and by some of his friends among the graduates. Two reasons were given: the students had not been given sufficient training to take any responsibility for other people's children; the intrusion of students upon town areas would be resented by town folk. Mills did not believe in field work at the undergraduate level. Today his department and several others are actively engaged in field work, and generous grants toward the work have been made by educational foundations of the highest reputation. The town's reaction has invariably been favorable. Indeed, nothing has counted so much in breaking down the prejudice against the college as a place of idle snobs and impractical idealists, as the field studies of its students and their subsequent interest in its welfare.

In the prohibition days a certain roadhouse caused much trouble. I went to Judge Morschauser about it. He said: "You can't get a conviction here in Dutchess County on a liquor charge, but I'll tell you what to do. You see Judge Medalie of the Federal Court." I took his advice. The Judge sent up a pair of Federal men, who did a strong-arm job on the mirrors, furniture, and fixtures of the roadhouse. It was, in fact, so well done that the proprietor, who had recently moved into the neighborhood, and who was sure some powerful rival in his field was after him, moved out as quickly as he had come.

One of the Indians was a Federal income tax inspector, John D. King. He had a baritone voice as big as the bulls of Bashan, and sang "My own United States" till the Catskills echoed. Franklin Roosevelt appointed him his official singer of that song, on a convivial afternoon at the Washington Hollow Fair Grounds.

Visiting firemen from Kingston and Fishkill were not wanting at the clambakes, nor were the aristocrats of River Row, the Rogers, Dinsmores, Dows, Roosevelts, and others. Lee Wager, local humorist from Rhinebeck, was a favorite of all, a natural humorist with a flavor like Mark Twain.

One night we celebrated the victory at the polls of Judge Young, distinguished jurist of our district. Nominated on both tickets, he had been unanimously elected. The hit of the evening was Wager's speech, telling how Judge Young came to Rhinebeck to solicit his vote, and was beguiled into drawing up a chattel mortgage on a cow, too difficult a law case for Lawyer Wager. Thus fortified, Wager, who had never, by his own admission, done a unanimous thing in his life, voted for Young, and the day was saved. After thirty years, the speech remains the wittiest I ever heard, and a masterpiece of American local humor.

"I'm getting absentminded," said Lee. "My sister said yesterday: 'Lee, I want you should go to the store and bring a yeast cake and a crate o' beer,' and I plumb forgot the yeast cake."

Lee Wager's yeast cake was proverbial in Poughkeepsie parlance for many a day.

John Mack and his sister Margaret, the first citizens of Arlington, are good neighbors. Their mother was on the college staff. John became a famous lawyer and Federal judge, and put Franklin Roosevelt twice in nomination for the presidency. Miss Mack treasures her friendship with Eleanor Roosevelt. From the beginning of our life at Vassar we became friends, Judge Mack warmly approving our efforts to make Vassar a good neighbor.

At a dinner in honor of the Roosevelts, John Mack told the story of the old squire who lived at Millerton and who was investigating the merits of the newfangled telephone. While putting in a call to his wife in Poughkeepsie a bolt of lightning hit the line, knocking him clear across the room. "That's Maria all right! I'll take it," said the squire. Pointing to Eleanor, John Mack said, "We all love Franklin, but we *know* Maria."

Judge Mack led the movement to keep the village of Arlington from incorporation in the city limits of Poughkeepsie. Thus the Vassar farms are in the city, but the college lies outside its boundary line. The "town of Poughkeepsie" lies north, east, and south of the city, and has gained in population very rapidly, while the city has scarcely gained five per cent in thirty years.

Dr. Taylor's "Vassar" does not mention the city or town of Poughkeepsie except in passing. Nor does Miss Haight's book on Matthew. It was a part of the fear at the time that Vassar College, in active competition with the New England colleges at Northampton, South Hadley, and Wellesley, and with Bryn Mawr in its aristocratic suburb, would not win the fickle favor of the public because Poughkeepsie could not be looked on as a favorable place for a college. Hence, I think, the constant depreciation of the city in Vassar girls' talk, and the restriction of social intercourse. Like all restrictions of the kind, it made the pursuit only the more sporting, and many Vassar women married the local jeweler, or clerk, or carpenter, just to show how love could still laugh at locksmiths. In residence of alumnae Poughkeepsie stands third, ahead of Chicago and Boston.

In point of fact Poughkeepsie was a most favorable center for a prestige college. The county had a large and famous group of

New Yorkers, whose estates lined the Hudson and stretched far inland. The De Peysters, Crugers, Livingstons, Montgomerys, Chanlers, Astors, Dows, Rogers, Vanderbilts, Roosevelts, Pells, Thornes, Towers, Flaglers, and the rest, were a society not to be overlooked. Vassar began to make friends with them, and our timid overtures brought a little response. The old families came to recognize that there was a college near by, at least. A few of the younger ones came to the Vassar Horse Shows.

There were some exceptions. Mrs. Richard Aldrich of the Astor-Chanler families, became a kind and helpful friend. Mr. Dows and Mr. Roosevelt became trustees. Mr. Henry Morgenthau Jr. and his wife (V.C. '13) were more frequent visitors. But the old rebuffing attitude still persists and has hitherto kept Vassar from the fullest employment of her exceptionally favored environment. I had no interest in encouraging the patronage of those wealthy families, unless somehow I could bring in the local people of the villages and farms, as well. To some extent we succeeded in this. Music brought in the local schools, art the local painters. The college set aside a part of its farm for an experimental orchard, under the State Agricultural Station. We had a local "school day" in the Circle. The Norrie Fellowship in half a dozen studies surveyed the county. The Social Museum attracted attention with its local exhibits of housing. Vassar fostered a dialect map of the region. Botany students prepared an ecological map of the county. Students worked in the Community Theater. A general disposition of good will was developed awaiting a vigorous drive to make the neighborhood know the college as a neighbor. But the final steps were still to be taken.

BUSMAN'S HOLIDAYS

COLLEGE PRESIDENTS WITH BRIGHT new academic gowns love to march in academic parades. College junkets take up much of their lives. I learned in my first year, and even before my own very pretentious inauguration, that I might easily spend all my time a-junketing.

Moreover, college presidents are great joiners. They love to belong to the innumerable associations of do-gooders. An Oxford professor, Sir James Craigie, once said to me: "It is better to do well than to do good," and I took it to heart. I tried to keep my name off petitions to the President and the Congress, avoided press releases, and came to regret the times when I weakly consented to talk for publication. It is very gratifying to realize that one's name is important to somebody. I learned, however, that it is the name of the college that counts, and that I had no right to exploit it.

So I made the opposite mistake. I stayed at home too much. As member of the American Council on Education, the Association of the American Colleges of the National Education Association, the Association of the Colleges and Preparatory Schools of the Middle States and Maryland, the Association of Colleges of New York State, and all the rest, I was inconspicuous by my absence, and soon forgotten. I was well scolded for it by my friend James L. McConaughy, President of Wesleyan, afterwards Governor of Connecticut. He pointed out that a college presidency was often the road to political advancement, as in his case.

When an upstate university invited me to become its head, Henry Morgenthau, Sr., advised me to accept.

"You are a Democrat. We need good upstate Democrats. Get busy up there and you may be Governor some day."

I had the compliment, after retirement, of being asked to run for Congress from my district. As no Democratic Congressman from Dutchess was ever elected since the memory of man, the invitation was perhaps not too alluring. I pleaded age and health, and sincerely so. I had no illusions as to my abilities in a political way, at sixty-six.

One association, however, proved most fruitful. The Association of Four Colleges, whose origin at Vassar has been described, was a meeting of executives on common needs and purposes. President Burton of Smith was eager to "modernize" Smith College. President Pendleton of Wellesley was a keen and unsparing critic of the inadequacies of college education, and especially of its low standards. President Woolley of Mount Holyoke was a great figure in the world of women, a great speaker on moral issues, and an advocate, almost to the point of martyrdom, in the cause of peace. Moreover, they were all good companions.

We met twice a year, weekending in rotation at our colleges. Each of us served in turn as chairman. Soon we added our Deans, and a member elected from each faculty. The Conference became a training-school for me as the numerous problems of college administration were taken up and discussed. Presidential aspects were separately discussed, but the Presidents were also most talkative at regular sessions. We also chose the most comfortable seats.

"Presidents gravitate to plush," I observed at one session, and the faculty members agreed.

In my experience in men's colleges where I had studied or taught, New York, Harvard, Yale, Columbia, Chicago, the factor of competition had seemed strong. Fostered by intercollegiate athletics, the rivalry spread to all departments. There was almost no intercourse among them, but an abysmal ignorance of the general scene of American education. A visit as occasional lecturer at Yale was a revelation to a Harvard professor. Here was another university of which he had never heard. He couldn't believe his eyes. It was amazing.

The women's colleges were more cosmopolitan. Already women collegians had shown their ability to cooperate. The Association of Collegiate Alumnae, in starting which Vassar's Abbie Leach had had a leading role, was not duplicated by any similar association of men. Under its present name, American Association of University Women, it is still without rival.

In their modest back seats, scarcely known to the general public in any accurate way, the women's colleges had decided to hang together, so as not to hang separately. As a newcomer, I had started with some acquaintance of them. While a graduate student at Harvard, I had friends at Wellesley, one of them, Sally Eustis, president of the student body, a neighbor and playmate at University Heights in the Bronx. From her I learned real respect for the fairness of women students in questions of authority. While teaching at Smith, Marjorie and I had become good friends of Miss Woolley at South Hadley, just across the Connecticut River from our home. She was a grand person.

So I seconded the conference with all my heart. We soon answered our most pressing needs for exchange of information, and looked about for some concrete project. The problem of admission presented itself. None of us were satisfied with the method of entrance by certification of the school principal. It did not occur to us that it was a good method wrongly used, nor had we the means at our disposal for its improvement, for personnel psychology was then unknown to us. Obviously, the right thing to do was to abolish the certificate, and replace it with the examinations of the College Entrance Examination Board. Was it not sanctioned by the prestige of the Big Three of the East—Harvard, Yale, and Princeton? Within a few months we had taken our plans to our faculties, and the change took place. It cost us the goodwill of the western high-school men. At a meeting in Chicago, the bitter resentment at eastern domination of education flared out in an angry denunciation of the whole plan. Later, we modified our scheme to follow Harvard's lead again in admitting students high in their class to enter on certificate.

I am sorry that we did not, as Sarah Lawrence did in 1927, adopt a personnel program, for the examinations did not prove very accurate, and the principal's letter of recommendation, whenever it entered into any detail at all of personal analysis, still proved much the most accurate rating so far as borne out by the college record. But at least we had the satisfaction of doing just as the "best" men did. The schools, too, appreciated the uniform systems of registration, which made work easier for them.

Admission on advanced standing was also started by the conference. Vassar never profited much by it, for the faculty did not want students from other colleges. They were, perhaps, too critical. We assumed that Vassar education being the best of all possible educations, four years of it was the highest privilege; and so long as enough freshmen turned up, why bother with later students, no matter how good they might be?

The social side of the Four College Conference was quite as valuable as the formal one. Good relations in administration were followed by cooperation on departmental and student levels. Vassar's intercollegiate conference on self-government, one of the first ever held, was a recognized part of the Fiftieth Anniversary. It lasted two days, under the gracious chairmanship of Irmarita Kellers, V.C. '16, President of Student Government. Tall and beautiful, of great dignity and presence of mind, her figure remains among my most vivid memories of the college.

Dr. Neilson's delightful personality soon succeeded to the forceful drive of Marion Burton. The Conference, enlarged by Neilson's influence to seven colleges, took over the task undertaken by the presidents, of presenting the claims of women's colleges to a fair share of the major benefactions accruing to education. Millions of dollars have come to them as a result of this effort.

Neilson's magnetic powers of attraction were illustrated at a meeting at Wellesley. We were given a room in the President's House. Dressing for dinner, Neilson discovered that he had forgotten to pack black shoes. They were always patent leather for dress in those days.

"I'm going to wear my yellow ones, and see how long it will take the delegates to spot them," he said.

We went down to dinner, greeting the nineteen delegates with more than usual effusiveness. Both then and at table, and at coffee afterwards, Neilson was the life of the party. His sallies sparkled with wit, and were the cause of unwonted wit in others. Not one of the nineteen noticed the bright yellow shoes until Neilson sat down at the chairman's table to open the meeting, and nonchalantly crossed his legs with a conspicuous swagger. Then a shout of laughter confessed their unobservant failure.

On a bright spring afternoon, Mildred Thompson, the Secretary of Admissions, and I set forth for Smith to attend an early meeting of this conference. She was to present the report on the new plan for admission by examination. I was to speak at Smith chapel. It was one of those early thaws, and the unpaved highway between Lakeville and Great Barrington was a slough in which we mired fast. It took me a couple of hours to find a farmer who was willing to haul us out with his ox-team.

By seven, when we should have been dining in Northampton, we were rolling over the upper part of Jacob's Ladder, the steep road leading from the Berkshire hill-top down to Springfield. Here was no thaw. Great snowdrifts lined the highway; and into one of them we slid smoothly and firmly. There was nothing for it but to look for another farmer. The scene, as I learned, was Green Lake. Above it was a single farmhouse, that of Mr. and Mrs. Fred Brodie. I knocked, explained our plight to the kindly farmer, and persuaded him to pull us out with his team. All this took a matter of two hours more. We decided to return to Pitts-field, leave the car, and take a train to Springfield.

So back to Pittsfield we went. By this time our Vassar Secretary of Admissions was beginning to feel a frog in her throat, what with sun, mud, snow, and ice. Arrived at Pittsfield, we learned that no train was due till half-past two. As I put the car in a hotel garage, a man drove in. His car was snow-covered but otherwise clear. He told me he had just come up Jacob's Ladder, that the road was easy to use, if we had chains. Mildred was game to try it again, and so, with new chains purchased and tight on the wheels, we set forth once more for Jacob's Ladder. At the identical spot, believe it or not, below Fred Brodie's house, but this time on the opposite side of the road, we went clear off the road and into a snowdrift eight feet deep. The front half of the car was buried.

I knocked again at Fred Brodie's. It was midnight. Fred appeared at last, this time in red flannel underwear, peering at me curiously.

"Mr. Brodie," I said, "here is that same —— fool you helped before. We're stuck again in the same place."

He said no word, but went to dress. This time he couldn't help us, but a man a mile down the road had a car that could take us back to Pittsfield. So, once more, we traversed the weary snow-lined road.

"Didn't you make a wrong turn?" I asked at one point.

Our driver stopped his car.

"Young man, I am supervisor of highways of this town. Judging from your performance tonight, and from my position, which of us is likely to know the right road to Pittsfield?"

Well, we got to Springfield at a quarter to five, and to North-ampton at eight. No sleep all night. Mildred was voiceless, and I was dead tired, and showed it. Our colleagues looked at each other, but said nothing. What Dean McCaleb thought when I slept on her shoulder on the train back to Poughkeepsie she kept strictly to herself. I got the car back, four weeks later. The incident was kept secret by Mildred and me, but I am sure it became a part of the legend of the new administration.

Though impatient of most intercollegiate gatherings of my colleagues in administration and instruction, I was eager to help students in their efforts by intercollegiate action to promote the setting up of student government in other colleges. I talked of it early and late. Through suggestions of Vassar women I was asked to address the meeting of the Liberal Clubs at Harvard, where the problem of student life was fully explored. Out of it came the National Student Federation of America, whose meetings at Princeton, Michigan, and Toledo, and elsewhere I attended. I helped to draft their constitution, but with this task I withdrew, since they were now ready to paddle their own canoe.

By 1922 I was so interested in this problem that I spent a sabbatical semester studying student life in Central Europe. Visiting Frankfort, Berlin, and Königsberg (probably the first American lecturer in Germany after the war), Copenhagen, Oslo, Göteborg, Lund, Stockholm, Upsala, Abo, Helsinki, Reval, Dorpat, Riga, Kovno, Vilna, Lwow, Warsaw, Krakow, Praha, Pilsen, Bratislava, and Brno, I met student officers in all of them, and discussed their problems. In each university, on the invitation of the "Rector Magnificus," I addressed the faculty on American university life.

I pleaded everywhere, to deaf ears most of the time, for recognition of the students' Bill of Rights—his right to his share in the administration of the university. I urged the moral responsibility of the university for the student's whole life, and the unwisdom of leaving him, unorganized and idle, to be the prey of unscrupulous demagogues. Even as I spoke, German students were attacking their own Jewish classmates, and their professors looked by on the other side. Students were sharply divided into political parties. Under such conditions the Nazis and Fascists, and Communists, too, made all too easy converts, in the very centers of university life from which our own system had come.

I attended two world meetings of the C.I.E. (Confederation

Internationale des Etudiants), and two sessions of the World Federation of Educational Associations (Edinburgh and San Francisco). Almost never did I meet another American college president at any student meeting, though they were always invited. I came reluctantly to the conclusion that American administration at the time was simply not interested in students, except as sources of tuition. My article in the "New Republic" on the "Students' Share in College Government" was not approved.

The final sin in their eyes was the meeting of the World Council of Students at Vassar in 1938. There the communist infiltration of student life was fully exposed, but all that was done was to condemn those who exposed it. No reaction took place until the Second World War to show our slow realization that wars were begun, and revolutions gained, in the classroom, some years before the outbreak of hostilities. My experience from 1915 onward led me directly to this conclusion, that study, not agitation, was the proper role of the student.

To Mr. George A. Dimock, the chairman of our Executive Committee, I suggested in 1922 the promotion of an intercollegiate conference on trustee administration. The idea was endorsed by Julius H. Barnes, one of our trustees who offered to bear the expense, but received no other approval, and was dropped. Some years later, Lafayette College established its well-known conference, which has more than fulfilled my expectations. Vassar trustees have regularly attended.

In an article entitled "Parents and Students" in Harper's Magazine I called attention to the lack of any real criticism of our college system, and invited it. It came fast enough thereafter, though probably not at my rash invitation. Experiments in new kinds of colleges were rapidly undertaken, at Antioch, Hiram, Albion, Rollins, Wisconsin, Sarah Lawrence, Bennington, Bard, St. John's, and elsewhere. Most of them are flourishing today on the experimental basis planned twenty-five years ago. At about the same time the great universities began to stir in their slumber, and to revise their curricula.

If one could generalize on this whole period one might say that the idea of a college, so often attacked, was found to be good. Courses needed to be revised to take realistically into account the nature of the freshman in America, to coordinate the particular sciences and arts into a view of art and science as general ways of looking at life, and to introduce the student to his own society. Administrative procedure was revised in the interest of promoting maturity and self-reliance. Basic fields were set forth as preliminary to all special studies, while at the same time by improvements in the method of instruction students were found ready for much more advanced and more independent work in their junior and senior years. At the same time students became more conscious of their own responsibilities. In all these movements the Vassar group took an active though not a leading part, held back by tradition, by interest, and by its modest place among the colleges. Yet to live in that era, and to share in it, if not "bliss" or "very heaven," in Wordsworthian phrase, was still exciting and compensating. The reaction against it came in World War II, with the return to the out-moded idea of a uniform program.

Most important of all, it seemed to me, was the student's response, not only when confronted with her own small segment of the universe, but when faced with her own shortcomings. Many went through a religious experience and set their feet on good camp ground. For others the change was to come later, but at least they were made conscious of the need. Others began to build their philosophy of life, to choose their field, to espouse their cause, to see how long a way they must go in order to reach their goal. Direction, perspective, foresight; with some, insight, and inward grace. It was hard to stand by and let them wander, but my own uncertainty did not make me a trustworthy Mr. Greatheart. I could only hope that somehow they would reach the Interpreter's House, somewhere along the way.

FLING THE BANNER WIDE

PROMPTLY AT 6:30 the train rolled into the station. It was still dark at midwinter, but in the smoky dressing-room, where the buzz of three electric shavers had silenced all wish to exchange greetings with my fellow-passengers, I regretted now, that I had forgotten President Hadley's parting word of advice: "Always take a drawing-room; you will then be fresh to greet your alumnae."

No porter was stirring at this hour, of course, and I lugged my two bags up the long stairs, where the glad-eyed graduates awaited me. The silent husbands snatched the bags from willing hands, and silently stole away to the parked cars, while their wives fell upon me.

"How are you, Prexy? I'm Eileen Bidford, '13. My, it's good to see you. And how is Vassar? Let us see; I have not been back since 1914; that was before your time, was it not? Where were you yesterday? Oh, yes, at Minneapolis? Did you see Peg Douglas there? She has had measles, you know. At her age. Is it not revolting? And you go there, tonight? To St. Louis? Have you your reservation? Do you not want to stop at the Pullman window to make sure everything is clear? Yes, I am sure you do. There it is, over on the side. Johnny, stop pulling my dress. We will have breakfast as soon as we get home. I hope you are not tired. My, it's good to see you. Old times are best. Not but that my husband and all are not just lovely. Were you ever here before? Well, I'll tell you all about it when we get in the car. There's the car now. John! John! here we are. Now, Prexy, you get in first. Johnny, sit up with your father in front. There we are. All right, John, now we can go."

It is restful. Silently I obey. As I sit down and relax against the cushions, I catch Husband's eye in the driving-mirror. It winks, and I wink back. All is well.

"Of course Sally Crittenden should have had you for breakfast, Prexy, because of course she's chairman of the Vassar Branch, but of course she has four sons, and I have three daughters, so of course that makes a difference; and I wanted to talk with you about Emmy Lou. You see, she's just no good at languages, and the Committee, the mean things, wrote to her the other day and told her she'd have to take an exam in Latin, because her school marks weren't quite high enough in it. Don't you think that was mean, to snoop around and pry into her weakest subject? And you know the catalogue says Vassar is interested in a girl's special abilities. It doesn't say anything about a girl's disabilities. Then why does the Committee—"

"Margaret, suppose we leave Emmy Lou's Latin till after the Doctor has had his breakfast."

"Oh, yes, John, that reminds me. Prexy, I hope you don't mind, but I've asked a few neighbors in to breakfast. They're not Vassar or anything, and they haven't any daughters, so you can just relax and be friendly. Everybody says you're so delightful at meals. I know you will just scintillate, and I *did* want my neighbors to see our Prexy."

Husband pulled up at the curb.

"Here we are, at our cozy home. The girls are all asleep, so I'll just take you up to your room, and you can rest till seven-thirty, when we'll eat. And I'll just go over your schedule with you. We do not have a college president every day, you know. Although Miss Perkins, she's the headmistress of Plugaway Hall, that's our girls' school, you know, over on the hill three miles out of town—it used to be poor Mr. Scheffelhauser's estate, you know, the one who financed the treasure-hunt in the Straits of Magellan last year? He lost all his money, and died very suddenly, but I always thought—well, anyhow, Miss Perkins says you will be the sixth women's college president in two weeks to visit the school, and if your speech today is going to be "What Makes an Educated Person?" she will faint and the senior class will riot. So please don't talk about education. They just want to see you, you know; that is what makes a girl make up her mind which college she wants to go to. That is what I did, anyhow. Dear Prexy Taylor came out here, and he stood up and just twinkled with those wonderful eyes of his, and then he saw me looking at him. I guess my mouth was open or something; anyhow, I just *adored* him, and he laughed right out, such a jolly laugh, and I decided that it was Vassar for me, and it always has been Vassar. I'm not Phi Beta or anything, and I know I'll never set the Mississippi or whatever it is on fire, but I have three girls for Vassar, and that's doing something, do not you think so?"

"About the schedule—"

"Oh, yes, the schedule. Well, we go first to Plugaway and then—why do we bother with it now? It does look awfully long and complicated, although I *tried* to keep it short and simple the way you asked me. But I had a lot of social obligations to pay off. You know how it is. I got John Cowper Powys for our Tuesday Reading Club on condition that you would speak at the Old Ladies Home on 'The Good Old Days.' I hope you will not mind. It is so easy for you, and they will get such pleasure out of it."

So came breakfast, with stewed peaches, cereal, and fried chicken with buckwheat cakes, and the neighbors. If I didn't eat everything my hospitable hostess had prepared, there fell an expression of such acute physical pain over her anxious face that I hastily picked up knife and fork and went on gorging, while the talk flowed on. Then with a cheerful honk Leila Buckington arrived with her shiny roadster, and off we sped to Plugaway Hall.

A girls' school in the Middle West had a not too easy time of it. The great high schools gave it no quarter. It was "undemocratic," the product of the leisure class who wanted their daughters brought up in Eastern fashion, free from contamination with the vulgar run of citizens. Any suggestion that the purpose might be to secure more personal training, a somewhat stricter standard of achievement, and a fulfillment of the requirements, however unreasonable they might be, of Eastern colleges, was greeted with incredulity. Usually the attendance was small, and the tuition low, for the family ambitions were not commensurate with their income. Yet they struggled on, and if the headmistress was a woman of thrift and determination as well as a good judge of teaching, might last a generation. Then either a generous patron endowed the school with a fine new building, and perhaps a productive fund, or the school closed, until another effort was made to fill the mild demand.

I saw many of them in my early trips from Santa Fe to Bangor, and from St. Augustine to Seattle. Many of our best students came from them, not too well prepared in some cases, but eager to justify parental hopes, and usually succeeding. Of the more than two hundred students from the Middle West, almost all came from the private schools of the region.

Wealthier girls went to Eastern boarding schools, at least for the two later years of school. Some of the few high-school graduates did the same, but most of the high schools frowned on the practice.

Vassar, with "democracy" in her tradition, tried hard to woo the high schools. Graduates wanted their principals to know that although the private schools had a right to exist in the "Valley of Democracy," there was no feeling of superiority. Many of our graduates served on boards of public education, and devoted themselves to securing better teaching and adequate equipment. Memphis and Little Rock I recall as outstanding instances of cities where Vassar graduates had given wholehearted support to local high schools.

On the other hand, many principals were not averse to

showing their great schools, with thousands of pupils, to Eastern visitors. They were proud of the great work that was done. Often these schools were far better built, and more modern in appointment, than any New England college could boast. I well remember a day in Des Moines with John W. Studebaker, who was to be my successor as national director of the Junior Red Cross, and later the United States Commissioner of Education. We visited one after another of the great high schools, taking in classrooms where significant experiments were being tried. Studebaker was himself a teacher of mathematics, with an enviable reputation for the introduction of new methods in the oldest of studies. One came to learn and to admire.

These thoughts came after the return. The hectic day under alumnae guidance left no time for them. From school to school we sped with my demon chauffeur, an alumna just out of college, and eager to show the paces of her new Maxwell roadster. I have had some narrow escapes in my life, and have been in real danger more than once, but never so often or so long as when seated with alumnae drivers making a morning schedule from school to school. Miss Buckington races across from North to South and from East to West High, some sixty-odd miles, although the red lights stop her, nothing else. Sheridan at Winchester is nothing to her. She goes twice as far and five times as fast, but the victory is doubtful.

One of the talks is a débâcle. I had arranged to speak with lantern slides on "Campus Life," and had brought some lovely pictures by George Shattuck, our teacher of geology, who was, indeed, so skillful as a photographer that he later resigned from Vassar to take motion pictures of wild animals in the African jungle. He had, also, at my fatuous suggestion, taken pictures of the college in its business aspects. In my innocence I hoped the trustees would enjoy them. By mistake they were in my slide-box, in a section alongside the pictures of students at play and at work.

Why tell the rest? I went out on the vast stage and was introduced by the principal, after a few songs and cheers for the football team. The girl in the lantern booth picked up the box, and upset the whole set of slides. Then in a panic she began to rush them through. So as I began, "Matthew Vassar, in 1861," out came on the enormous screen a picture of a great Holstein bull. A roar went up. I clicked the signal, and began again: "The Vassar student body"—out came a herd of Holstein cows, climbing over each other in their haste to get out into green pastures. The hall went hysterical. One after another, pictures of chickens and pigs, boilers and ice wagons came pelting along.

I rushed from the stage and climbed up to the booth, where a crying girl was slipping in slide after slide. Forcible restraint was the only means of stopping her. The principal turned on the auditorium lights. A howling mob of high-school boys and girls tottered off to class. I never saw that high school again.

At the others I did my best with little talks whose only merit was brevity. They were apprentice pieces and should never have bored an audience. At each school a few girls volunteered to meet me after the talk, and asked sensible questions, such as: Why go to Vassar, when we have good colleges in this state? I talked on national unity, on Washington's hope for a national university to help in bringing it about. Their eyes brightened when I casually referred to West Point and other colleges nearby. They could see some merit in the idea.

At least I did not speak on "What Makes an Educated Person?"

Miss Buckington's tour ended at lunch time, when I was delivered to Mr. Bidford, who had, under I know not what threats from home, secured my admission to a luncheon of the Queer Dick Club, the most exclusive circle in the city. They were progressive in some ways; they had adopted the custom of wearing big disks on their lapels with their first name printed in large letters. One labelled "Henry" was promptly affixed to me, and I was Henrified for the next hour most diligently.

Called in for a four-minute talk after other guests had

spoken, I tried to say something that would offend nobody, and so though I talked four minutes, I said nothing. I had forgotten my little pack of joke-cards, carefully written out and classified by Miss Marks, after I had culled them from my reading. Not one could I recall, and I sat down without a sound of approval.

"Doctor, there are a few reporters Mrs. Bidford asked to see you today. They're waiting outside. Miss Adamsapple will be here in twenty minutes to take you to your next appointment." Mr. Bidford, with the air of Christian when his burden fell off, hurried off to his office.

"How do you like Nebraska? Are you married? Have you any children? What does Mrs. MacCracken think of your teaching girls? Why does a woman's college have a man president? Don't you feel silly teaching women? Why do women go to college, anyway? How do you keep them at work? What is the present status of the sex problem at Vassar?"

Knowing nothing about sex whatever except what I read in Chaucer, I haven't much to say, and the interview is soon spent.

"Now, Doctor, if you will just stand in the corner, I promised Mrs. Bidford I'd try to get your picture in our paper. It won't be easy, but she has promised me an exclusive for her garden party if we would print it, and I think I can fix it with the desk."

Miserably unhappy, I stagger to the corner. Sure enough, three weeks later a clipping bureau sends me a photo of a scared rabbit with my name underneath in mercifully small letters.

"Ruth Adamsapple, Nineteen Five. Now, boys, hurry it up. We have a full day ahead."

A businesslike young woman of my own age takes my arm competently and steers me out of the interview with a genial word to the reporters, who look almost as relieved as Mr. Bidford.

"Mr. MacCracken, there's a lot of anxious mothers who want to talk to you about the new admission requirements. They are scared to death of these examinations. They judge their children by their own work at college, and can see nothing but failure ahead. Come on, cheer them up. They are in my office on the seventeenth floor of this building."

So off we go. On the way up a friendly hand slaps me on the back with a "Hullo, Professor, I heard you were in town."

"McCreery!"

"That's right. Bill McCreery, Yale '12. Remember good old Division 7? You bet us we would lose half of the division by Easter, and we all passed. You paid up, too. You said I was the dullest brain of the whole division."

"I'm glad to see you, McCreery. Is your office in this building?"

"No, I own it. This is the McCreery Block. Just collecting rents. Well, so long, Professor, nice to have seen you. You did a lot for me."

Eight mothers awaited me at Lawyer Adamsapple's office. They would hardly wait to be introduced before they flung themselves at me. Questions rattled like hail on the roof, and no one seemed to listen to the answers. A comforting word or two was all I could get in. By this time my brain was weakening, and as I looked at them all I could see was our herd of cows, horning each other as they pushed out of the barnyard. I tried to banish the image in vain. Twenty minutes of torture, and Miss Adamsapple showed them out with good-natured urging, and a promise that everything would be all right. She had their addresses, I would look up everything when I got back, and write them all about their daughters.

It was my turn to look relieved. Miss Adamsapple took one glance at my face and laughed heartily. "A tough assignment, Mr. MacCracken. Never mind, you'll get used to it. All this folderol is utterly useless. I cannot see why they sent you out this way, anyhow. Only one girl a year goes from this town to Vassar, and wild horses couldn't keep her off the road to Poughkeepsie. What do they think college is? A day nursery? If they'd just leave their little darlings alone, they would do all right. But no, they must all pass, no matter how dumb they are, just to keep up their own self-esteem and their social prestige. Wouldn't do to have a daughter fail at Vassar. That would be just awful."

We talked a little about Middleburg, and her law practice. She was doing well. She asked after Miss Salmon.

"There's a teacher for you. Never paid any attention to a college bell. I can't remember a thing she taught us, but somehow she made me see myself in all my crudity and immaturity, and made me want to do something about it. If it weren't for her I wouldn't be here, but she wrote me you would be out and asked me to do what I could. Come in the inner office a minute, I have something that's good for corns."

We silently toasted Miss Salmon.

"Excuse me, Miss Adamsapple, a lady to see you."

"Hello, Pinkeye, how's tricks? Mr. MacCracken—can't think of you as Prexy yet awhile—this is Martha Frauenfeld, our leading citizen."

"Nonsense, Jo—"

"Yes, you are, now. One of them, anyhow. She's our Commissioner of Highways, and a darn good one. Does more work than any three men in the state."

"President MacCracken, you must not listen to her. You're due at McWhorter College, anyhow, and I have promised to get you there early to meet Dr. Foxfield."

"All right, take him along. Goodby, Mr. MacCracken. Hurry back."

"Shan't I see you at the alumnae tea?"

"Not me, never go. I can represent Vassar on my own occasions."

McWhorter College and President Foxfield were not so terrifying as the rest of the day. The college let me off easy with a talk on teaching literature to their English Department, and Foxfield I found a thoroughly good sort, a plain man who knew exactly what he was doing and what he was up against, in trying to bring a small denominational college upwards and outwards, as the copybooks might say. But the respite was brief. Mrs. Frauenfeld carried me smoothly and swiftly around the grounds. She was a trustee, it appeared.

"It may seem strange to you, Dr. MacCracken, that a Vassar woman should put in most of her spare time trying to help another college to get on its feet. But that's what Miss Wylie taught us, you know, to pitch in wherever we were and get things done. You know how she always talked! 'Go on, yuh silly girls! Yuh can do it, yuh know yuh can!' She did a lot for me in building up confidence, and living as I do over a thousand miles from Vassar, I feel I'm really working for her right here."

Dr. Foxfield, at any rate, thought it an excellent idea. "Mrs. Frauenfeld is my good right hand. We shall name our next building Frauenfeld Hall."

It appeared that Vassar women were of many kinds. Partly because the ones I met were likely to be the ones that made good, it seemed that every one of them counted, in one way or another, in her community. I began to form the idea, which I never carried out, of changing the Vassar motto: "Purity and Wisdom" to "Valere" (to count). I asked Mr. Cole one day to make a seal with this motto. He did so, etching it in wood from a Greek statuette in Mrs. Elon Hooker's possession, of a lovely young winged goddess lighting on a cloud, with a little pennant displayed: "Valere." I have it yet.

But the afternoon rolled along, and here we were at the Vassar Tea. It was a doublebarreled affair at Mrs. Frank Nickerson's, a beautiful English style manor house picturesquely landscaped in the best part of town. Mrs. Nickerson was cordial and charming, but everything was in pastel, compared with the rest of the day. Part One consisted of fifty or sixty mothers and daughters, the confident carefree ones. Everything was for the best in the best of all possible colleges. The girls enjoyed the album of Vassar pictures. I talked to them a little about Vassar life, and tried to answer many questions. A beautiful tea was served just as Vassar alumnae began to arrive. It was like any tea the world around, but rather better—everything exquisite. Then the mothers and daughters faded away with much good will and infinite content, and left the world to Vassar and to me.

What a session that was! I made no speech, just answered questions, amounting to three speeches at least, for an hour and a half. They wanted everything changed; they wanted nothing changed. They wanted Vassar to teach housekeeping; they didn't want it at all. They debated everything. No two agreed, but they did not balance out. Most of the time I was a looker-on and a listener-to, occasionally on appeal getting a chance to wedge in a point or two.

At least it was heartening to see that these women took seriously the meaning of education in their lives. Most of them obviously kept up with the times on modern ideas in education, as much for their children as for their own interest, no doubt. One or two only were in opposition, and came with bees in their bonnet or bats in their belfry. Vassar was radical. It made women unfeminine. It was unhealthy. It overdid its health work. "I lost my health at Vassar." What did it do with all its money? Why did it not pay its teachers more? And so on and on.

But for the most part it was an enlivening meeting of minds, with good will uppermost. Then, when I began to look white about the gills—I had been under fire for ten consecutive hours—I was whisked off by Mrs. Bidford to dress for dinner. On the way home she told me stories of the love life of her fellow alumnae, very spicy, some of it.

Just as I started to dress came a knock at the door. "I'm sorry, there's another reporter, a woman who does features for the Sunday paper. She wants to do a little article, and just can't wait."

So, in Mr. Bidford's dressing gown, I tried to talk about education in as literate a way as I could. Education to me was learning something. The question was what? Well, the best, you know. What is the best for you? You have to find out what's best for you. So you sample. Of course you want to learn what you don't know, not what you do know. But there is no end to

learning, even if you know a little. Eventually, you find you want
to know more of what you know already, and then you stop
browsing around. College is the place where you do that, etc.,
etc. She took it all down in shorthand like Bill the Lizard as long
as her ink lasted and then borrowed my fountain pen. I shivered
to think how it would look in print, but at least it couldn't do
any harm, and a nice picture of Taylor Hall would make it all
right. So I talked away, and was as dignified as I could be in a
dressing gown twice my size.

Dinner followed at Mr. and Mrs. Girald Montesquiou, you
know, the Frenchman with an English mother, who came over
to play polo, and married the daughter of the buckwheat king!
She didn't graduate, of course, but she had the nicest house in
town, and was on the finance committee of the club. She was a
friend of Mrs. Van Boskirk, the aged widow who sat at my right,
and was obviously to be deferred to. She could give you a dormitory, if she wanted, right out of her purse.

So the pleasant masquerade went on, an innocent pastime
enough, surely, with the irony of the situation not too apparent.
The talk was good among the husbands present, and when they
talked the women who had talked so trippingly fell suddenly
silent, as if they lived in two worlds. There was little of the give-
and-take of a dinner in England, but rather a series of excellent
monologues. There were cocktails and wines, and I was very careful, but I got so sleepy I could have laid myself to rest upon any
bosom present. After dinner the men gave me a good going over.
Vassar as a business was reviewed from the farm to the president's salary. When I told them I received six thousand dollars
they glanced at each other. Their head clerks got twice as much,
of course. At any rate their questions died down as the ash
lengthened on their cigars, and we turned to politics. I was glad
to be left to obscurity.

We joined the ladies—there was much good-natured joking
about women, women's colleges, women's ways in general. It
struck me that the sexes in America were very badly adjusted to

each other. They didn't respect each other, really. Always uneasy together, always tension.

But there was no time for further talk; goodbye all round! Such a pleasant day! So grateful for everything!

Mr. Bidford took me to the midnight sleeper for St. Louis.

"Doctor, how long have you been out?"

"Well, let's see, this is Saturday. I started on a Saturday, Syracuse, Buffalo, Detroit, Saginaw, Grand Rapids, South Bend, Chicago, Milwaukee, St. Paul, Minneapolis, Des Moines and here. Then I have St. Louis, Louisville, Cincinnati, Pittsburgh and home. Sixteen in all. I've made fifty-four speeches so far."

"Doctor, I don't see how you do it, I don't see why you do it, and I don't see why they make you do it. I wouldn't wish a trip like that on one of my salesmen, and they wouldn't take it. Yet all you college presidents do it year after year, Lowell and all of them."

"Well," I reflected, "it's lots easier than staying at college. I always feel rested after a trip."

The alumnae solicitude followed me back to campus. A worthy graduate from Cleveland called on Marjorie. "Mrs. Mac-Cracken, your husband went all around Cleveland with his shoes unpolished. They looked so uncouth. Things like that always reflect on the wife, in the long run. Of course I realize you weren't there, but, still, a wife's influence goes with her husband everywhere, I always say."

They taught me patriotism. On the morning which witnessed America's entry into World War I, a little old lady came into my office.

"Dr. MacCracken, no flag is flying on this building."

"I'm afraid that is something I have overlooked. I'm not sure, even, that Vassar has a flag."

"Oh yes, it has. I am Mrs. Thomas McGraw, Vassar 1867. Three of us survive from the day when we entered Vassar at the end of our great war. We have not forgotten those days. My son, Capt. Stanley McGraw, is downstairs with a United States flag, and will now raise it. I invite you to accompany me to the ceremony.

"But before we go, here are 1867 dollars to endow the American flag forever at the Main flagpole. Use surplus income as you please, but keep the flag in condition and always have one in reserve."

Four periods of Vassar women can be easily observed. Mrs. McGraw belonged to the "strong-minded" women, who claimed equality of mental powers with men, and who insisted that good minds were meant to be used. Of such was Mrs. Edwin Abbey, wife of the famous artist, who declined her father's offer of a costly coming-out in Boston society, to teach in a city school, and who fell in love with a struggling artist and married him, like the princess in the story. I came to know her well, and to visit her at her home in Chelsea by the Thames. In her will she left Vassar two hundred thousand dollars to endow the president with a ten thousand dollar salary, for she thought he was underpaid. Unfortunately, her death occurred in the great depression, and the estate could not produce the sum. I was grateful for her kind intention.

Then there were the "dangerous" women. Harriot Stanton Blatch was one of them. Mrs. Blatch took lunch with me on her fiftieth anniversary. "It seems strange," she said, "to be in the President's House at Vassar. For many years I was banned by my own college. I could not speak on the campus. We were regarded as unworthy of our education, and now the cause we fought for has become the law of the land."

There was still about her a spice of the old intrepidity and a cool irony in her talk. She was not fooled by our deferential courtesy, for she knew how much was still to be won.

After the "dangerous" came the women of Dr. Taylor's creation, the "well-rounded" women. They were to be "leading" women, taking a part in all civic enterprise without ever losing their charm. Well rounded indeed, for they were exceedingly well fed in his days, and they burst out of their Gibson girl stays like lilies on their slender stems. A little of this, a little of that, but nothing too much in the way of study. Some of them took one elementary course in each of twenty departments.

They were prosperous days, the Nineties and the Nineteen Hundreds, and they were complacent as well as well rounded, healthy and happy folk, and much to be envied. Some of them became aware that the world wasn't mostly as they thought it was, and did a good deal about it. Of such was Frances Jewell, '13, the Kentucky dean who married her president and chose Sarah Gibson Blanding for her successor in the deanship. A dynamo of energy with a clear analytic mind, she combined the intrepidity of the strong-minded and dangerous ages with the charm of the well rounded women.

How shall I define this later crop of graduates, since 1915? The earlier types persist among them, and in goodly numbers. But the horizon perhaps is broader, and I might venture to call them "liberal" women, without shooting too wide of the mark. Liberal in every sense they have proved, generous in giving themselves, hospitable to new ideas and experiments, learning through friendship with foreign students how to overcome the old barriers in human relations, enlightened in social problems, and free to take up the struggle for justice which is the human task of our age. And still able to laugh at themselves.

> Oh, the daisy-chain marshal wears a rose and gray dress
> That cost a million dollars, not a cent more or less!
> (The Post inserts this item, as it gallops to press.)
> *Vassar song.*

Let me be quite serious for a moment.

A college runs on four wheels: students and teachers are the front wheels, hitting the bumps, feeling the way; graduates and trustees (for the public) are the big back wheels. They carry a big share of the load, take the brakes when they are needed, and encourage the front wheels "keep on, we are right behind you." The president? Well, he is a sort of postboy, riding a wheeler.

I believed deeply in the value of bringing in the alumnae to share in forming the college policy. They are consular officers accredited to the younger generation. They help to support the college. They should have the privilege of electing a good number of the trustees. But since their interest in exercising this privilege is not too strong, and the number of voters is small, the trustees should also choose additional graduates, to represent nonvoters as well as voters. Thus through their trustees, their own officers, and their public relations, they may make their wishes known.

Two resources are needed to sustain such a program: continued education and inspired leadership. I really mean education, not promotion; more knowledge about the whole world of thought and action. A sustained relationship with one's college may become the most rewarding kind of adult learning.

As to leaders, the 50th Anniversary in 1915 discovered them for Vassar. They were such women as Constance Rourke, Amy Reed, and Helen Kenyon. Constance was the chronicler, Amy the general chairman, Helen the hostess during that famous week in October. It marked, more than anything else, the rise to power of a really organized alumnae body. Constance became a leader of American thought; Amy became the leader of the faculty; and Helen became the leader first of the alumnae and then of the trustees for twenty-two years. It was fortunate for me that this leadership came in my first year before it had crystallized. We could work together from foundations to superstructure, experimenting as we went, but never in conflict.

PUBLIC RELATIONS

MATTHEW VASSAR BELIEVED IN ADVERTISING, and paid liberally for it, in magazines, newspapers, and posters. The trustees of later days followed him rather timidly. They bought space in "ad" columns, and they encouraged stories about Vassar in the better magazines. That young women had healthy appetites was news; the magazines printed pictures of long lines of waitresses bearing trays heaped high with pancakes. This great discovery is still news, as I found when I casually mentioned that Vassar students ate five barrels of apples when apple pie was on the card.

It was news also, when young women enjoyed themselves at college. Somehow this thought seemed to threaten the idea of the male's indispensability. Girls couldn't *really* have a good time by themselves. What about feminine jealousy, quarrelsomeness, gossip, and selfishness? Was it not well known that women dressed only for men, that nothing kept up their morale except the thought of pleasing men? The rapid deterioration of women who lost their feminine charm in an atmosphere exclusively feminine was the myth of the age. The debate still goes on. It was a Vassar woman of 1916 that wrote "Women Are Here to Stay."

People read with avidity and unbelief the word that women remained women where men were not around. They learned, and doubted, that men were not particularly welcome at women's colleges. "Men are dear beasties, but oh, not at college," one Vassar story affirmed. The magazines printed pictures of tree

167

ceremony, ivy planting, hoop rolling, and even a Vassar May Pole. The daisy chain, that threatened in the 'Twenties to bind Vassar publicity forever in its golden bonds, was not known to the American public until the Nineties. Vassar fudge, brought to the college as a southern recipe, was known far and wide among young people, but I have never seen a reference to it in print. A fountain-pen company published a photograph of Vassar's library in a harmless ad, but the trustees made the photographer suppress it. Vassar chocolates were more defiant, and the college learned that it had no copyright on the name unless the word "college" was attached. At my first visit to Kansas City the manufacturer of Vassar chocolates presented me with a five-pound box, in pure goodwill.

In Poughkeepsie, the Vassar tailors, laundry, theater, shoe shop, grill, and other shops flourished. Vassarettes and Vassar shops made sales in cities from coast to coast. The Vassar Old Men's Home, Vassar Brothers Institute and Hospital meant more to most Poughkeepsians than the college, and to this day the word Vassar in a Poughkeepsie headline means the hospital of Matthew's nephews, not Matthew's darling college.

In my earliest attempt to tell about the college I learned very soon that American men were entirely indifferent to the idea of equality of the intellect. College women were therefore freaks, amusing when not charming. They printed with scorn the statistics of the marriage rate among college women, entirely regardless of the fact that college men rated no higher in the scale. At the time, 1915, this rate was about 50%, the birth rate among collegians being rarely more than one child in a family. All this, of course, was blamed on education. This failure in biological terms was the most frequent objection to college for women. At an alumnae luncheon in New York a well-known psychiatrist, a woman, tackled Marjorie about the matter. My wife was tired of the subject already, both because she had mothered four children while the psychiatrist had none, and.

because she was not a college woman herself. She therefore replied that she did not believe in accepting the dictates of biology, whatever that was; that the human race had made a mess of things so far, and that it would be a good idea to give it all back to the insects again, and let them have another try to evolve a better race than ours. At the close of the dinner the psychiatrist came to me, and in the most solemn manner asked me whether I had ever had my wife under psychiatric care. When I replied that I had not, she urged me to insist upon immediate examination, for my wife was in a most serious condition. It seemed like a joke, but I found she was in dead earnest, and was quite determined to save what remained of Marjorie's reason.

There was, of course, some ground for concern, if the assumptions of the biologists were to be granted. These were: that brains were the exclusive possession of the upper class; that brains made money, and hence the money group and the brain group were practically identical; that the country would have no brain group if the money group died out. All of which was pure assumption without a shadow of proof. Without knowing anything about it, I thought the biologists were all wrong, and said so. France, the most intellectual country in the world, had had a stationary population for a century, and still led the world in art, literature, and philosophy. The causes of population growth seemed to me social rather than biological. Economic factors were important, not just high or low wages, but the whole set of economic life. In America fierce competition and crowded housing in cities made children a nuisance. The wealthy classes found them a drag on their favorite pastimes of travel, sport, and night life.

Beginning about the time of emancipation of the slaves, the women's rights movement gathered momentum. It was a symptom of women's dissatisfaction with the conditions of women's life, including marriage and marital conventions. Celibate life, independent careers, increase of divorce, limitation of children, were all, or seemed to be, evidence that the American family needed attention.

In one of my first addresses, I described the Founder's concern with the life of women as women, and the need of studies in this field. Mrs. Hadley heard this speech and urged me to approach Mrs. John Wood Blodgett (Minnie Cumnock '84) with a view to her becoming a trustee. As the lifelong friend of Ellen Richards, founder of home economics, of Julia Lathrop, founder of the Children's Bureau, and of Katharine B. Davis, leader in prison reform for women, commissioner of charities in New York and a leading authority in social hygiene and family physiology, Mrs. Blodgett had dedicated herself to this cause.

She did not require much urging, and with her entrance into the Vassar school began our work in Euthenics, the insistence that human relations were not solely controlled by environmental conditions, and that such control as environment exerted could be modified by human effort.

Vassar's only reference to the child in the catalogue of 1915 was a course in "Genetic Psychology, A study of behavior in the lower animals and the child." Today the Department of Child Study is a favorite in the free choice of students as a major field of interest.

The public relations attending Euthenics were amusing. Some critics, like Dr. Flexner, fell foul of the word. Dr. Flexner maintained that it was pure waste to teach a woman about children. She could learn all she needed to know in a week. It was not a fit subject for college, anyhow. He derided it in his comparison between American and German universities, which had no child study.

Others, almost equally offensive, cried: "At last! women are coming to their senses!" This aroused the militant feminists and suffragists, who thought that we were trying to drive women back into the home, and who insisted that the home required no mental skills. Considering modern statistics of industrial production, and the amount of money and time spent by men engineers on the home as a building, it might have been assumed that the *life* in the home would repay study; but they never changed their minds. Similarly, when I tried to explain to the American public the uses of Alumnae House as an informal graduate school, where women scholars could live while working in intellectual studies, the reporters immediately doubted it. "The School for Bored Wives," and nothing I could say would stop it.

In other words, the sex conventions governing our press were fifty years behind the times. Their attitude toward women pretended to be hardboiled, but was in fact merely primitive. There was not a hint of equality in it. In spite of the Nineteenth Amendment and all it implied, American public opinion was influenced towards a sentimental view of lord-of-creation stuff. The sex drives today are further stimulated by the psychologists who control most advertising, in the direction of sex urges, to a point where we are the laughing stock of Europe, and most of all the Soviet Union. Acting on this discovery, I gave up trying to use the press for an intelligent presentation of what went on in women's colleges. Analyzing my problem, I found that we had four audiences who might be expected to read about Vassar, or to hear about it. These were: girls looking toward college, and their parents; the learned professors and educational foundations; the readers of non-fiction magazines and books; and the Poughkeepsie community.

In my first year of office I experimented by inviting Burges Johnson, a former editor of Harper's Magazine and a well-known writer. Burges soon became a college feature. His office in Main Building became the center of the literary life of the college, a life that I found mature and dynamic. The Vassar *Miscellany*, later the *Miscellany News*, was one of the best college periodicals. In its pages many young writers had found their start. Several undergraduates had already been passed from its pages to the magazines. Margaret Leech was then a junior. She later was a Pulitzer Prize winner. Elizabeth Coatsworth was a senior. She wrote charming and witty verse, and later catered to the juvenile public, winning a gold medal as the best juvenile writer of the year. Caroline Link was a sophomore. She published thoughtful and sincere poetry of a social quality. Vincent Millay, '17, already known before her entrance, was writing brilliant sonnets. In the literary group more honest and outright thinking was being done than elsewhere in the college, it seemed at times.

In his "Well of English and the Bucket" Johnson summarized the experience of a hundred and fifty students who later earned money by their wits and their pens. He showed clearly the value of college work in English in perfecting their tools and their skills. Some of them, like Julia Coburn, '18, became editors of leading magazines; others went into publishing work and into advertising; but many were successful in fiction and poetry. "Jane Clare" was the pseudonym of two roommates who began to write after leaving college, and whose novels have been successful both in print and on the screen.

Johnson's work was outlined for him in Public Relations, Publications, and Publicity, in that order of importance. He kept the local press on good terms; and for the first time events at Vassar were clearly and accurately reported in Poughkeepsie papers. We began to build up a public for our offerings in music, art, and the theater, and for our lectures and preachers. Instead of the impression of an exclusive college, the notice of a friendly place that was a part of the community began to spread. The activities of our professors in local societies were made known. The Dutchess County Health Association, first of its kind in America, the local visiting nurse association, the Historical Association, under Dr. James F. Baldwin, the Associated Charities under Professor Mills, the Women's City and County Club under Professor Wylie, the Community Theater under Professor Buck, the Vassar Brothers Institute under Professor White— these and many others, being publicized, elicited an editorial in one paper pointing out that the best contributions Vassar College could make to its community were the lives of its professors. For many years Professor Fite represented the district in the legislature.

Johnson encouraged professors to write, and helped them to sell their wares. The *Yale Review* and the Sunday literary sections of the New York papers, published many articles on college education in general and on women's colleges in particular.

For the Fiftieth Anniversary seven books were published at the cost of the college. Margaret Washburn's "Movement and Mental Imagery" was perhaps the best of these, but Eloise Ellery's "Brisson" and Caroline Furness' "Variable Stars" were highly praised.

I began to see that our faculty had in its members the potentiality of successful university scholarship, and all that was needed was encouragement. So, when Lucy Salmon brought me her manuscript on "the history of the press," I labored to help her bring it into shape, and secured from an alumna the fund for its publication by the Oxford University Press. It was natural, then, when she retired, that the fund raised in her honor by her pupils should be directed at her death to the encouragement of faculty research and publication. Other publication funds and research aids followed. Today it is doubtful whether any other college is better equipped for the encouragement of genuine scholarly work.

I found, also, that the old slander against American Ph.D.'s was entirely false. It was sneeringly said that students got the Ph.D. only to get instructorships, and that once won, the Ph.D. meant nothing for further work. What I found was that the instructor was overloaded with work as compared with the professor, that she was likely to be in debt for the cost of her studies, and that further publication seemed to her out of the question.

Obviously, the first step was to equalize the teaching load so that instructors taught no more hours than professors. Next, a careful review of the instructor's studies and interests was made, and encouragement given to further research. Finally, by grants in aid, by purchase of books and equipment, and by special leaves on faculty fellowships, the way became clear for early publication.

The attainment of all this was of course a matter of years, but its beginning lay in public relations, in my attempt to interpret our teachers and their work to the college public.

At the Fiftieth Anniversary I suggested to the alumnae the establishment of a quarterly magazine which should tell this story to our graduates. The suggestion was immediately taken up. The quarterly still appears, as the Vassar *Alumnae Magazine,* a periodical of enduring quality and value. From the beginning it published articles of broad educational and social interest, for I hoped for it a public like that which Professor Wilbur Cross, my old Yale colleague, had won for his *Yale Review.* That goal was never reached, but the Vassar *Magazine* has succeeded in leading Vassar graduates to think of their college and of their own education as bound up in the world's welfare.

To aid our professors in their professional fields, we made it possible for them to attend professional meetings through contributions from college funds. In short, life in the faculty became itself a training for better professional work and standing. The reputation of the college rose accordingly, and the daughters of our leading educators attended Vassar in large numbers. I remember once boasting that the heads of Yale, Cornell, Princeton, Pennsylvania, Illinois, Colorado, Michigan, Minnesota, Purdue, Wisconsin, Case, Syracuse, Pittsburgh, Amherst, Williams, Wesleyan, Skidmore and Beirut had Vassar daughters. It was a silly piece of bragging, but it did reflect not only a certain social trend, but a recognition of the estimate by experts of our faculty's quality.

Along with aids to professional development went training in administration. Here again recognition followed upon our plan of giving every instructor a faculty vote, and an opportunity for administrative work in committees and bureaus. In later years Vassar faculty and Vassar students served Wellesley, Connecticut, Sarah Lawrence, and Sweet Briar as presidents, and Wellesley, Radcliffe, Smith, Mt. Holyoke, Russell Sage, Barnard, Bryn Mawr, Goucher, Stanford, Minnesota, Sweet Briar, and many others as deans. The meetings of headmistresses seemed almost to be Vassar reunions. This was not accidental, nor do I in setting it down seek to claim credit in any way. Many of those women were at Vassar before 1915. But the record does seem to show that in some way Vassar encouraged the growth of character and leadership, and that in some way this fact became known in the educational world. So keen was the Vassar scent for public relations that shortly after a famous inventor came out with his denunciation of college women a Vassar girl married the inventor's son.

Those were the days when Calvin Coolidge wrote of our blasting at the Rock of Ages, and called our colleges dangerous, when Vassar women led suffrage parades on Fifth Avenue, and chained themselves to the White House fence. But they were also the days when over a hundred and fifty of them went to France for war work. Burges Johnson taught me to get over my fears and worries about single items about Vassar women in the public eye.

"Look at these clippings," said he. "Here is a sample month. Here are six hundred items of news in which the college is mentioned. More than half of them are about nice girls, as Dean McCaleb calls them, marrying nice young men. That is publicity that counts, and you don't have to do anything about it except to graduate nice young women."

As an example of the skill with which we suppressed news about the college, I may add that my own misadventure in 1918, to be related, though known in all its aspects to several thousand Vassar students and graduates, never reached the press. Inaccurate rumor reached the ears of Upton Sinclair, however, and he described the event, attributing it to President Meiklejohn of Amherst. As for me, though he mentioned me in other connections, Sinclair always referred to me by feminine pronouns.

When I wrote him about it, he refused to believe that I could be a man. I offered to go to California at his expense and prove my maleness, but he refused the bet.

The persistent depreciation of American education, and of women's colleges in particular, was a characteristic of the time. America was just beginning to shake off the collar of provincialism, and to find itself. I remember well the day when Livingstone Farrand, president of Cornell and an expert in medical education, said to me: "The time has passed when an American medical student needs to study abroad."

Dr. Abraham Flexner's book, "Universities, British, German, and American," did immeasurable harm in giving Europeans warrant for their sense of superiority to us in educational matters. I engaged in something of an educational controversy with Dr. Flexner, for he had failed to mention women's colleges in his book, except in passing. The controversy reached the printed page and offered a chance for the women's colleges of America to throw down a gauntlet to European education, a challenge that was not taken up.

I asked why, if European education was superior, we could not find teachers or students in Europe who would come to America and win our fellowships. Vassar was generous in awarding scholarships, and in welcoming foreign students, but although she had fifty students from abroad every year, none of them reached our highest standards. Most of them, we found, had to learn how to study after they came. Their records were on the whole good but not superior.

Foreign teachers, likewise, did not, as a rule, seem to know how to teach well. The number of those who could deliver a really good and "gisty" lecture, to use the Smith word, was very limited. Vassar has been hospitable to foreign scholars, its faculty holding degrees from thirty foreign universities, but these teachers were not markedly superior to the rest.

I offered the evidence of our language work, because Dr.

Flexner had said we did not know how to teach languages in America. He declined to examine it.

Finally I suggested to the faculty that we publish some of the papers written by our students in their regular class exercises, and submit them to the criticism of a candid world. The result was the Journal of Undergraduate Studies, which even Dr. Flexner could not refuse the title of creditable, while the *New York Times* commented editorially upon the quality and style of the papers. Nothing, I think, did more to raise the opinion of the judicious concerning the quality of our education. Many of the papers served as base for dissertations on the level of masters' and doctors' degrees. But what was much more important, it taught our students that we believed in and honored their work, and found it worth publication.

Such activities led to a larger controversy, the quality of work in women's colleges as compared with that of men's colleges, and the corollary attendant upon it, that if women's colleges were equal to, or superior to, men's colleges in quality of work, they deserved equal support. This campaign, which lasted several years and brought much honor and some money to the women's colleges, was carried on by the Conference of Seven Colleges, itself the outgrowth of the Four College Conference at Vassar, 1915.

My own field was mediaeval English literature. I found at Vassar a group of teachers interested in the period, and to them I suggested a volume of Mediaeval Studies, following the Fiftieth Anniversary series. This was taken up, and the result was a handsome volume, with a number of important articles. The object of my suggestion was to break down departmental lines, and to show the number of fields of study in which the mediaeval period had much to teach us.

The interrelation of fields of study was a favorite theme of mine. When the Sanders Laboratory of Physics was dedicated, a week's lecture-institute was held on the theme: "Physics in its

Relations." It was honored by the most famous American physicists. We published the lectures.

Whether, beyond all these forms of publication, a continuous and vigorous drive on the newspaper public will bring results to colleges, I am by no means certain. I am not of those who believe with Jesse Lynch Williams of the Princeton press bureau, that "all news is good news." I cannot believe that the reading public is as stupid as that. But discontent with our more limited forms of publicity has always existed at Vassar. In my first year I met alumnae who complained that Barnard filled the New York papers, and they never read about Vassar. That seems to me a childish attitude, and a costly one.

The sensational drives might bring results, but I was certainly not the man to head them. To manage our public relations so as to keep on good terms with our town, in good repute with those in our profession, and with good will among those who in some way wish to know about Vassar, was all that I could hope.

Within the college, to stimulate original intellectual activity so that throughout its membership there was the sense of something stirring, seemed to me the aim in my own field of public action. To that I addressed myself with enthusiasm. It was not spectacular, but it moved.

One of the most successful campaigners in public relations of those days was Mrs. Percy V. Pennybacker, whose daughter Ruth was a Vassar student and a good friend of ours. Mrs. Pennybacker was a permanent feature at Chautauqua Assembly. She was an eloquent speaker, able to hold vast audiences enthralled. I sighed in vain to possess her gifts, although she very kindly encouraged me.

Once, at the annual meeting of the General Federation of Women's Clubs, of which she was president, I was asked to address an audience of seven thousand women in the Seventh Regiment Armory in New York City. Vast bleachers had been put up on the armory floor. Opposite them, on a high throne sat Mrs. Pennybacker, whose slight form could hardly be seen at the distance. Her voice, penetrating at all times, resounded in thunderous tones, reechoed from every wall under the drive of powerful mikes.

Augustly she declaimed my turn to speak.

"Mrs. John V. Blank of Pittsville has been given four minutes in which to introduce the next speaker."

Twittering and bridling like a chickadee, Mrs. Blank mounted the sacred steps to a minor rostrum.

"The Pittsville Federation of Women's Clubs has enjoyed a most favorable year," said she. "We have held numerous meetings of great importance, and have adopted resolutions on child care, social welfare, and many other subjects of the highest interest. Our committees have worked hard, and the attendance has been most gratifying. I was very much embarrassed when they elected me the president of the Federation, for I felt that my experience was insufficient and my abilities inadequate for so important an office."

So she sang on, until the four minutes were gone.

Bang! went Mrs. Pennybacker's gavel.

"Sit down, Mrs. Blank! Your time is up!"

"But, Mrs. Pennybacker," wailed Mrs. Blank, "I haven't finished. I've only begun."

"Sit down, Mrs. Blank. You were given four minutes, and you have used them."

"But I can't sit down, Mrs. Pennybacker, I've got to introduce Dr. MacCracken."

"Sit down!"

"I won't sit down. I came all the way from Pittsville to make this introduction, and I am going to make it."

Bang, bang went the gavel, this time as loud as a bomb.

"The Secretary will read the rules, section XIV."

The Secretary read section XIV, which set forth that during annual meetings the President of the Federation had absolute authority for conducting the program on scheduled time.

"Now, Mrs. Blank," came the thunderous voice, "for the last time, sit down."

Bang, bang!

"Boohoo," said Mrs. Blank.

At Mrs. Pennybacker's nod, I arose and became the sacrifice. What I said I never knew.

RAISING THE WIND

THE SOLICITATION OF FUNDS is a business, a racket, a technique, a sport, or an art according to your point of view. Whatever it is, it is deeply embedded in the American way of running things. It's an old business—witness Chaucer's Pardoner.* The Pardoner knew all the tricks of the trade; how to appeal to the fear of social loss, to individual pride, and to "something for something."

It is not a business for the sensitive, or the shy, or the impatient. It is, I think, only endurable when it is taken as a sport (stalking deer is the nearest parallel) or as an art.

As a profession, fund-raising is wholly in the field of public relations. The so-called fund-raisers raise none of the funds. They make surveys of need and prospects, prepare circulars and pamphlets, organize directories and files, teach methods to workers, and then watch the money roll in. They fulfill a function like that of a life insurance company which for a slight fee of 14% teaches you to be thrifty, careful, or provident, or leaves you, rather, to be your own careless self, while assuming these virtues for you. The fund-raiser, for a variable fee, puts you to work to raise funds and exploits your lower motives of sport, excitement, power, and even competition in a race for a goal against time and the hardened heart.

The years of my term have witnessed great gifts for educa-

* Boweth youre heed under this hooly bulle,
Cometh up, ye wyves, offreth of youre wolle!
Youre names I entre heer in my rolle anon!
Into the blisse of hevene shul ye gon!

tion, and Vassar's increase of assets during my term from five million to twenty-five million dollars in endowment and plant only kept her in her place as a prominent woman's college. Relatively, indeed, she rather lost ground, and largely, I think, because I never made fund-raising a primary concern.

In their plans for the inauguration of the young president, the trustees graciously allowed him one place in the program. It was the personal speech of the occasion. I chose Professor Kittredge, asking him to repeat an address he had given at a teachers' smoker. He was the hardest man in the world to beguile into such a talk, but his friendship for his old pupil prevailed over his busy scholar's life, and he accepted. He called it "The Scholar and the Pedant."

He assumed that Vassar in choosing me had expressed its wish for a scholar, though it just escaped getting a pedant. Pedantry he defined as the technical language of somebody else, and humorously defended the right of any group, learned or not, to use its own vocabulary.

But though Kittredge assumed that Vassar had broken precedent in wanting a scholar as president, he was under no illusions as to the real nature of the job. That was, to raise money. Kittredge compared a president of a college to the parson in the Prologue to the Canterbury Tales.

". . . though his parish, like that of Chaucer's parson, is 'wide, with houses far asunder,' he is expected to visit them all, 'upon his feet, and in his hand a staff.' " He made no quotation, however, of the Parson's admonitory duties.

All too true was Mr. Kittredge. By stealing time from other duties, by imposing on good-natured colleagues who filled my place during my absences, and by catching up on the literature in my field during vacations, I barely managed to salvage a part of my time for teaching. I could not give extra time for conferences and the careful supervision which college students need in writing. My courses were therefore restricted to the intermediate group, and in that group I taught soon or late nearly every course in the offering. As the English teachers filled in for me, I returned the favor by taking their courses when their leaves came round.

With some outside help I managed also to put together my texts of Lydgate's shorter poems, and publish a volume for the Early English Text Society. A final volume in that series, on which I worked fitfully with the aid from a scholarly assistant, Mrs. Hortense Marks, is still in the clouds. While the world has not got on very well without it, it certainly would get on no better with it.

So I became a displaced person, a refugee from scholarship. I have to confess now, that I might have saved my time and strength for it. Administrative work is intensive, and to some extent seasonable. Most presidents take three months vacation, sometimes more. Some of them manage a month at Christmas, and a fortnight or longer in Florida in early spring, as well. They have plenty of time for scholarship if they choose it. But their work unfits them for it. They get the itch for the platform. It is hard to resist and it soothes the vanity. The introductions alone are worth the trouble, to one who needs a restorative to his pride and his conscience. He knows they are not true, but he likes the warm bath of flattery.

After all, was I really a scholar? A teacher, yes; but why had I spent so much time at Yale over textbooks, if my aims were really scholarly? Why was I so easily diverted into civic life, church work, and social reform? Though I worked feverishly in the rather barren field I had chosen, my grasp of it grew no stronger or wiser. I was not, by nature, gifted with a love for detail, and accuracy was never sure with me, nor systematic recording of my reading. I read too widely over the surface of all fields.

Though my friend at Harvard, William H. Schofield, lamented my defection from scholarship, I shed no tears. It was a good background for my life among the scholars of the faculty, but my pleasure in securing opportunities for the scholarly development of others was far greater than any pleasure I had ever had in the occupation.

When the alumnae, in my first month of office, proposed to me the launching of a drive for a million dollars, I was more than ready for it. The trustees had assured me that finances would not be my concern, that the alumnae had no such idea. Louise Sheppard, their spokesman, was one of our wardens, and lived in Strong House. Together we set up an organization, for it never occurred to us to seek professional aid.

Dr. Taylor had depended almost entirely on personal solicitation without publicity or organization. He had worn himself out in travel and correspondence, with disappointing results. During the three years previous, gifts to the college had not exceeded five thousand dollars in any one year. It was, he told me, his chief reason for resigning at the statutory age of sixty-five. A younger man must take on the burden. The college in his twenty-eight years had received as endowment less than a million dollars in all. Most of the money given in his time had gone for buildings to house and equip the rapidly expanding college.

Dr. Taylor, however, preached generous giving to a generation of younger graduates whose gifts came in later days. One of these gifts was the Vassar Alumnae House, presented by Mrs. Elon Hooker, '94, and Mrs. Avery Coonley, '96, in the spring of 1915, as a part of the Anniversary Fund. In the deliberate fashion of those days, nine years were to pass before the completed building was to gladden the hearts of alumnae. But the gift as well as the idea grew with the years, until it was many times the original amount.

Under the inspiration of Mr. Rockefeller's new policy of gifts conditional upon others, happier times were in sight for the colleges, Vassar among them. The Fiftieth Anniversary in 1915 furnished a good reason for a new appeal. So Dr. Henry M. Sanders, our honored trustee, and pastor of Mr. Rockefeller's own church, escorted me to the seat of the mighty, the "Rock-

(efeller) from which oil blessings flow," Dr. Sanders called it.

"Mr. Rockefeller," said Dr. Sanders one day, "you have made a scriptural passage very clear to me. 'The meek shall inherit the earth.' You are the meekest man I ever knew, and you have inherited most of it."

The General Education Board at 61 Broadway was our goal. Offices partitioned round a great central hall full of stenographers gave little evidence of the enormous power these men possessed. Dr. Gates (formerly a Vassar trustee), Buttrick (daughter Vassar, '17), Flexner, Rose, and the Auditor, Trevor Arnett, were the trusted almoners of the hundred and thirty millions then in the fund. These men were, I think, superior to their successors because they were less professional, and because religious and ethical grounds rather than scientific seemed to govern their actions.

They were prepared for us. Dr. Sanders was an old and trusted friend. We had in Dr. Buttrick's office the usual uproarious and jovial session that took place in those days whenever Protestant ministers met off duty. For thirty minutes they sat and cracked jokes, while I sat an amazed and anxious onlooker. Was this the consideration given to a request for a quarter of a million?

My question was answered at length, in one minute of serious talk at the end of the half hour, and we were dismissed. Dr. Sanders was in high spirits.

"You'll get it, or something like it, you'll see," he chortled. "They wouldn't have laughed so loud if they were going to hold back."

And so it proved, though the Board whittled down our request to two hundred thousand dollars.

On a later visit Dr. Flexner suggested that he was looking for something to survey, and would like to come up and survey Vassar. I welcomed the suggestion, but nothing came of it. Wickliff Rose, whose daughter followed Dr. Buttrick's to college, gave me a piece of good advice. "When you are hunting for money, use a rifle, not a shotgun. You'll be more likely to bring down your game."

I found this to be true, especially in appeals to foundations. These organizations, which have a preponderant influence in the development of higher education, were receptive to striking and original ideas, rather than to support of the general aims of a college. No prestige was involved in such a gift, nor any judgment rendered other than the endowment of a college as competent to manage its own affairs.

Only in the great gift of fifty million dollars, distributed in 1920 at the personal wish of Mr. Rockefeller, was any large sum devoted to the general aims of education. When the seven women's colleges asked for recognition, the Board singled out certain ones and denied the claims of others in a quite arbitrary manner. Our trustees at the time insisted on asking for a gymnasium, which was at the time our real need. This was refused, but a half million was given to Radcliffe for a physics building on the plea of graduate study, although at the time there were not half a dozen students in graduate physics. The story of American philanthropy has yet to be written. It is not to be found in the published reports.

Not long after my appeal had been made to the alumnae, an old Negro came to my office. He looked like an old family retainer.

"Have I the pleasure of speaking to Mr. MacCracken?"

"You are right."

"I was instructed to put this parcel in your hands. Will you please to sign this receipt?"

I did so and my visitor bowed out.

I opened the package, thinking it the manuscript of some book which an alumna wanted me to read. My eyes began to pop when a hundred thousand-dollar bonds of the Central Pacific Railroad and a check dropped out, making up the back value to the full hundred thousand. No sign of the giver. I could make my guess, of course, for I recalled the wonderful group of trustworthy attendants in the Standard Oil building, where Charles M. Pratt had his office. He was having his little joke.

I never had another one like it. But I once lunched with Mrs. Anita M. Blaine in Chicago, at the suggestion of her granddaughter, then at Vassar. "How much do you want me to give to the Seventy-fifth Chicago fund?" she asked.

"Whatever you will," I said.

A few days later Nancy Blaine told her grandmother I had devoted my birthday to the luncheon. Promptly came a birthday gift to me, an engraved cigarette case, and inside the case a check for ten thousand dollars.

As a rule, money was not thus played with. It was a most serious matter, performed sometimes with the solemnity of a rite. There came one day to my office Mr. Chester Pugsley of Peekskill, with his attorney. "Dr. MacCracken, I want your aid in a benefaction I am about to make, of half a million dollars." My spirits soared, but Mr. Pugsley went on. "I want your signature as witness to this deed of gift of five hundred thousand dollars to Harvard Law School for scholarships."

One of the greatest gifts in American education was recorded in the will of Margaret Slocum Sage. Her husband, Russell Sage, was physically unable to give money, and left it to his wife to perform. With the wise aid of Mr. Henry de Forest, she gave the great fortune to over fifty institutions, placing no restrictions on the gift. Professional almoners would have put limits upon it. Vassar's share, one unit of the estate, amounted to over seven hundred thousand dollars. Of this, the cost of Josselyn House must be subtracted, for when she gave this to Dr. Taylor, she deducted it from the unit left in the will. Vassar trustees set up the fund as a reserve for building maintenance and improvement, to be used and repaid from savings.

"I like to think of Uncle Russell Sage as coming to Vassar's help every little while, as he is needed, with the trustees to watch every expenditure." Thus said Russell Leffingwell, who had known the old and famous financier.

Mrs. Sage was a friend of my mother's. "What a pretty dress

you are wearing, Mrs. Sage," my mother said to her one day. Mrs. Sage began to weep. "I can't take any pleasure in it," she said. "Russell says I have a good dress already and shouldn't have bought this one."

I once accompanied my father in a call upon her. She had taken a small cottage in Lawrence, L. I., for the summer. Like other wealthy women, she felt hounded by charity-beggars, but endorsed us, since we came on no such purpose. The lot of the rich who do not know how to protect themselves is a hard one in America. I do not envy them.

Philanthropy in the grand manner was the hobby or rather the sport of Mr. George Plimpton, who obtained most generous gifts for Wellesley, Barnard, Amherst, and other colleges of his choice. The main building at Barnard is one of his prizes of the chase. On this occasion he chartered a yacht, and took a party of guests through Alaskan waterways. One morning Mr. Jacob Schiff came on deck and stood to view a great glacier, surrounded by lofty mountains. "At such a moment I am very humble," said Mr. Schiff. "I am deeply moved."

"Mr. Schiff, I know you want to remember this day by a generous act. You are going to give me a building for Barnard."

And so it came to pass, if we may trust Mr. Plimpton. Such strokes of the trustee were beyond my powers. Mr. Charles Wimpfheimer of New York gave Vassar its Nursery School after ten minutes' thought, upon my first meeting with him. I can recall no other large gift of such instant response. Doubtless he knew of his daughter's interest in child study. He had no other reason.

It was my experience that any large gift ought to be allowed to ripen on the tree, until ready to fall into Vassar's hand. Ten years, more or less, was the time required for the harvest. Knowledge of the college from one or more aspects, sharing its life from time to time, through trusteeship or alumnal office, personal friendship with students and teachers—these have provided the motives which in practically every case came into its fixed form as an original product of the giver's mind. I do not recall having actually asked for more than one. The idea of the gift came slowly, stimulated by numerous contacts. Some of the contacts were planned, no doubt, in the hope of awakening interest, but certainly they were successful in proportion to freedom from any appeal. In the case of those who were trustees, there was pretty full knowledge. In other instances, a single well-informed contact was enough to start the train of thought.

Consequently, if someone were to ask me, "How can I get large gifts?" I should have to confess ignorance. So far as I know, you don't "get" them, they grow out of experience. If you have the good fortune to work among people of means, the gifts will come. "Don't thee marry for money, but go where money is." Such is Tennyson's farmer's worldly advice.

But though these larger gifts stand out in Vassar's history, the small gifts far outnumber and outweigh them. My guess is, that gifts of a hundred thousand dollars do not come to ten millions in all, while the smaller gifts come to some fifteen millions at least. This estimate is based on cost of buildings at ten millions, not their replacement value. Not only are the smaller gifts, most of them at a hundred or two hundred dollars, more significant in the mass; they mean more to the college in other ways. Often fifty dollars is as much of a sacrifice as fifty thousand, in this country of ours. I think of the scholarship fund in his wife's memory built up by a missionary in India, in little savings, a few dollars at a time, through many years of service.

I think of a woman who came to my office one day in 1915, and said: "Forty years ago Vassar gave me a scholarship of one hundred dollars. It meant that I could keep on at college. I vowed then, that if I could earn the money, I would repay it a hundred fold. I have done so; here is my check for ten thousand dollars."

Only the condition of anonymity keeps me from giving the name.

There were many such gifts at the Fiftieth. It seemed as if

the alumnae were just waiting to be asked. Almost the whole correspondence was carried on by Louise Sheppard and her class secretaries. The fund of one million was oversubscribed within the year. Moreover, many gifts came later, inspired by the drive of the Fiftieth. The official Vassar seal of the year was a young and gallant maid, who replaced for the time the plump matron of the Vassar legal seal, who seems to be balancing herself on a part of the Yale fence, with a Yale "tomb" in the background. She seems to be waiting for a boy friend to come along.

"The new seal," said Marjorie, "means that Vassar is capable of rising to an occasion." And that it certainly did. The loyalty and dynamic drive seemed to grow year by year. When, in the war, a deficit was incurred, the alumnae paid it off in six weeks, with the generous aid of Mr. Pratt. Even without his aid, the graduates' gift was 80% of the deficit.

In 1922, it was the same story, when the alumnae gave two and a half million to meet Mr. Rockefeller's half million. Finally in 1940, the goal of two million was reached on the last day of the 75th Anniversary year. In none of these campaigns were professional money raisers employed.

Our professors shared in the drives. Margaret Washburn with her class in psychology organized a study of the emotional appreciation of music, and won a $500.00 prize offered by a phonograph company. It was Miss Washburn's subscription. I recall vividly how sure she was that she who had never done such an undignified thing would win the contest.

Our drives were valuable to Vassar leaders in training them for other social leadership. Many of our workers have become well known in different phases of American life as a result of this training.

In 1922, when Vassar celebrated the completion of the three-million-dollar salary-endowment fund, the commencement was uproarious in its jubilation. I apologized for it to our guests Sir James and Lady Craigie of Oxford.

"Don't think of it," said this worthy Scotsman and great

lexicographer. "Man, if only all my Oxford friends could see this, it would do them much good, and Oxford too." He laughed and sang with the rest over the victory for education.

A year later, in England, I was invited to a dinner in London, when I met the heads of the English colleges for women, and was closely quizzed upon the ways and means of getting support for women's education. I could not help them much. Later, at Edinburgh, I addressed the graduates' association, recently formed by a Scots professor whose American wife had taught him something.

In Praha three Vassar graduates obtained four million crowns to build the women's hall in the Charles University, with a gift from President Masaryk to start them. They obtained the rest by using their wits and their experience at Vassar. They were graduates of '22.

Among givers to Vassar none was more original than Mrs. Mary Clark Thompson, whose husband's portrait is above the fireplace in our library. I first met her in the 50th Anniversary year, at her home in Canandaigua. Later I was a visitor in her Madison Avenue home now replaced by a skyscraper.

Mrs. Thompson came of the generation of strongminded women, and shared their characteristics, though I think she did not go to college. Our professorship of political science was given by her at a trustees' meeting, in which Dr. Taylor had pleaded for its founding. As she left the room early, she put a slip of paper in Dr. Taylor's hand, stating that she would give the seventy-five thousand needed.

Her gift of the library wings was just as casual. It was contained in a tiny personal note, of the kind fashionable among young ladies at the time, and came in response to a brief note of mine, after my visit.

In art her gifts were not always welcome. Vereshtchagin's "Pearl Mosque of Agra" does not please the Art Department as much as it does me, and is very rarely shown. As for Houdon's bronze statue "La Frileuse," that is hidden in some subcellar, if indeed it remains at Vassar anywhere. Mrs. Thompson's famous collection of fans was not sought after.

The old lady was a great reader and a purist in the use of the mother tongue. My colloquial style needed much revision before she was satisfied with it. As soon as I learned of her concern about it, I gave her much material to work on. She enjoyed the task, and we became good friends. She left a curious, and for Vassar very unfortunate, will. After bequeathing Williams and Vassar Colleges each three hundred thousand dollars in outright bequests, she left the residuary estate to her nephews, to go to the colleges in case the nephews died without issue. The nephew was on Williams' side a bachelor, while the nephew on Vassar's side had three children.

The famous philanthropist Miss Helen Gould (Mrs. Finley Shepard) had endowed several women's colleges with scholarships, the recipients named by her. In each case the college was obliged to continue full board and tuition no matter what the rise in costs and prices. At Vassar this resulted in assuming a cost of $7500 for a $2500 benefit. The students named by her were not in all cases promising. Mrs. Shepard's hobby was the exposure of un-American activities. In the course of pursuing it, she came to think that all the women's colleges were hotbeds of radicalism, and announced her intention of naming no more girls to her scholarships. Vassar therefore offered her the option of returning her gifts, or of using the money in some other way at Vassar. She asked for the money, and it was repaid her, over $40,000 in all. The other colleges did not give her the option but transferred the funds to other uses. I was laughed at for our punctilio, but I do not regret our action.

The annual fund is a way of giving that came in after 1915. It is highly successful, though its cost of operation is considerable. Vassar's mass drives were given at a cost of three per cent on overhead operation, kept down by the large number of volunteer workers. Yet the annual funds are worth while as a means of continuing the interest of graduates, especially of those who live at a distance from the college.

On the whole the pursuit of wealth was as exciting as the pursuit of knowledge. I had few unhappy times. One man told me he would give a million dollars if I would tow Vassar down the Hudson out to deep water and sink her like the New York sewage. It had taught his daughter to think for herself, as he called it. She had gone to work in a store against his prohibition, and the college was to blame.

That same morning, in the office below this man's, in the same building, a man grasped me warmly by the hand in welcoming, expressed his gratitude to the college for all it had done for his daughter, and asked me to accept five thousand dollars. You can't please everybody.

With its endowment Vassar has over three hundred deeds of trust, the terms of which are published and periodically reviewed. The large number testifies to the number of interests at the college. "In memory of Professor Salmon's course in American History." "For Professor Dickinson's course in Music," is a gift by the young woman in whose memory the two million endowment in mental hygiene was recently given. The restrictions required a special budget for their faithful execution, but in the confidence which this gives to loyal graduates the cost is well repaid. At the same time unrestricted endowment is greatly needed at Vassar, and I doubt, sometimes, whether my encouragement of special gifts has been wholly wise.

THE TRUSTEES ARE THE COLLEGE

"WHAT'S THE MATTER with MacCracken?" someone asked Mr. Henry Pelton, Secretary of the Vassar Board of Trustees.

"Well," said Mr. Pelton, "he hurries me."

It was true. The speed of 1915 was not that of 1880. When I took office I had just passed my thirty-fourth birthday. The thirty members of the Board were sixty-four years old, possibly a little older. Thirty years makes a difference, when multiplied by thirty. Nine hundred years of cumulative experience was what I had to rush.

No man on the Board had any educational experience. They were ministers of the gospel, retired business men, bankers, industrialists, a hotel keeper, an insurance man. The ministers, three of them, were Dr. Taylor's classmates, with no particular interest in Vassar. Some of the business men were friends of the two men most interested in the college. One, a lawyer, Allen Evarts, was an old bachelor, who had once defended the college in a lawsuit over a disputed will. He lost the suit, and became a trustee. He was opposed to women's education, so far as I could learn, and voted against every measure proposed for its advancement. His two nieces were good friends of mine in student days, one of them, Josephine Evarts Tabor, an intimate family friend and counsellor. But that made no difference to "Uncle Allie."

The Board of thirty were self-perpetuating and the term of office was for life. They met once a year, on a June afternoon at Commencement time. The warm day and the hundreds of vis-

194

itors did not invite too prolonged consideration of college business. The President's report was read, the various committees presented the briefest of statements, the officers of the Board elected, and adjournment followed. The Board was absolute in its authority, and imposed no limitations upon its own actions. Bylaws and rules were unknown. A Green Book of Rules had once been adopted thirty years before, and then forgotten. The Board might at any time adopt any action it pleased.

All authority was actually centered in the Board's Executive Committee, which met at the college every month during the academic year. In the interim between its meetings the Chairman of the Executive Committee was the final authority on any matter not already included in its actions, and on the execution of any action authorized. The first action taken by the Board was to discontinue the practice of electing the president as chairman, and to choose Mr. George E. Dimock for the office.

I was assured that this action was taken in order to set me free for purely educational work. It sounded fine. My fear was relieved. I knew nothing whatever about finance or business. I couldn't even drive a nail straight. Manual labor I hated, as most scholars do. My exercise had been taken in sports, chiefly tennis. The only routines I knew were of the classroom and the library. So I willingly surrendered the authority of the president, never realizing that responsibility would be mine if anything went wrong. And that was my bane, as the Norse Saga says.

A local committee consisting of the three trustees resident in Poughkeepsie, who were also members of the Executive Committee, exercised a power almost as indefinite as that of its chairman. One of them, Edward Atwater, was chairman of the Finance Committee. As President of the Farmers and Manufacturers Bank, he held the securities of the college, invested its funds, and also carried the college account. A second member, John E. Adriance, retired head of a plow company, supervised the business administration of the college, all building and other construction, and was the man who knew which local firms

enjoyed the college custom. The third, Henry V. Pelton, was
secretary of the Board. He was a retired lawyer, who loved detail
for its own sake. In his secretarial capacity, he wrote all the letters
in the Board's correspondence. The minutes of the Board were
kept by him in longhand. He was also secretary of the Executive
Committee and of the Committee on Faculty and Studies, which
met with the President once a year, to talk over appointments to
the Faculty, and discuss the course of study.

Mr. Pelton had a very low opinion of women. It was his
chosen duty, at every meeting, to oppose the suggestions of every
one of the women trustees. Moreover he was the champion of
the status quo. Whatever was, was right. A man of great charm,
singular disinterestedness and high principles, with some literary
gift, and a real love of people, his legal training and his emotional
drives made him, as a Board member, an obstructionist.

He always spelled "allumnae." He did not approve of them.

The Board worked under no budget. The Comptroller took
in the money and paid all bills without any inspection. Mr. Polk,
the delightful Comptroller, received the list of officers from Mr.
Pelton, and the business bills from Mr. Gillespie, the Superintendent. As a professional buyer and steward, Mr. Gillespie was
efficient. He knew his business. The bills for tools and equipment, and all the costs of the departments of study, took him
beyond his knowledge.

Theoretically, all bills and purchases were approved by the
President. On my first morning in office a lot of cards were laid
on my desk for signature.

"What are these?"

"They are the books the librarian wants to buy."

"Do you mean I must approve every book?"

"Oh, yes, we are very careful about the choice of books. Dr.
Taylor did not approve of modern novels."

"Well, take them away, and tell Miss Reed never to send
them again. This censorship is abolished."

The minutes of the Executive Committee are full of such items as the following:

"The President presented the petition of Professor Marian Whitney for an additional electric light bulb for her department in Main Building. On motion the request was refused."

I was cautioned never to explain why a request was refused, never to defend the Board's action. How could I know the motives governing every trustee in his vote? But while professors were kept on a starvation diet in the matter of facilities, Mr. Gillespie could and did buy fifty thousand dollars' worth of coal without any supervision whatever, so long as he bought it from the old firm.

I was early the recipient of visitors from Poughkeepsie business men, who had not that stamp of trustee approval, and who hoped I might help them to get some share of the college business.

But presidential authority did not extend to this. The college was a close corporation, in which certain trustees had staked out their prerogatives. Women trustees like Julia Lathrop, one of our most distinguished public officers at the time, used to wonder what the new members had been elected to do. Not till after the reforms of 1918–22 were women trustees taken seriously. The real business of the college, its major and minor functions, were not written down anywhere, but just managed as matters of understanding.

One of the major items in a college business is insurance. Vassar's buildings and equipment were worth three and a half millions, and the premiums were high, since there was little that was fireproof. The business was in the hands of a preferred group of local agents. Mr. Dimock, after a pitched battle with the local trustees, placed the account with a New York firm, which exercised a supervision over the whole policy of insurance, although local agents continued to receive commissions. This was the first of many such struggles between the New York and the local trustees, which finally ended in the transfer of the funds to a New York bank, and the reduction of local trustees to one member, chosen for his efficiency as treasurer, with responsibility for the overall budget administration. That, however, was a matter of years.

The trustees of Vassar have all been honorable men and women of the highest standing. I never learned of any exception to this statement. I never learned that any trustee, local or national, profited in any way, personal or social, from any college fund or patronage. Mr. Atwater and his wife had given the college the Swift Infirmary, in memory of Mrs. Atwater's father, Charles W. Swift, a former mayor of Poughkeepsie. Mr. Adriance's family was a leading group in Poughkeepsie. The Adriance Memorial Library in the town is one of the best city libraries I have ever known. Every good work in town owed something to the Adriances. Mr. Pelton was utterly devoted to his community. A founder of the Amrita Club, the Tennis Club, and many other organizations, he was widely known and respected. What I have written here of the Vassar system had existed, so far as I know, from the early days of the college. It was, moreover, a general practice among American foundations. Management of large enterprises was a new occupation. It had not been developed professionally. Trevor Arnett's book on college finance, published some years later, was the first manual of college practice. It became the bible of college presidents, and its standards were made a condition by many givers, before their gifts were made.

I learned from Mr. Arnett about budgets, of which I had never heard. In approving the conditional grant of two hundred thousand dollars towards the million for Vassar's Fiftieth Anniversary Fund, Mr. Arnett made some inquiry about our methods, and shook his head. "You should operate a budget," said the canny Scotsman. I took this to heart. At the end of the year I wrote my friend and patron, Mr. Charles M. Pratt, who though he was not an officer of the Board, was the most generous contributor to Vassar at the time, and sat in MacGregor's chair. In my letter I urged the adoption of a budget. He approved, and the Board voted my proposal at the June meeting. Thereafter the educational budget was strictly operated on a budget basis, and no deficit was ever incurred. The rest of the college business went on exactly as before, until the Board reorganized its procedures in later years.

Theoretically, then, the Board was an absolute diarchy. In practice, of course, favored employees were completely autonomous in their own spheres. Miss Barrett, the Director of Halls, allowed no interference in her department. Mr. Stopher, the gardener, planted what he pleased in the garden, and harvested it when he deemed best. There was no dietary control. The chief chef was an autocrat. At any moment one of the "local" trustees was likely to turn up and exercise his authority. One day Mr. Stopher left his overseeing of the removal of a large pine tree in the south circle of Main Building, for a fatal interval. In his absence Mr. Pelton came by and took charge, and when Mr. Stopher returned the big tree had fallen smack against the building. No great damage was done, but it took many hours of the day to get it free. That wasn't the only time the college got smacked when a trustee casually took over.

Mr. Law, the boiler-plant engineer, was the most autocratic of all. He carried in his head everything known about the heating system, and when, one day, he was insubordinate in a talk with Trustee Adriance, and was summarily dismissed, that knowledge went with him. We had no blueprint of the water, gas, electric, sewer, or other systems. Leaking mains made themselves known by sight and by smell, but not otherwise. As a single sample of the inefficiency of the plant, we spent more for coal in 1918, I learned, than we did twenty years later, although we then heated and lighted twice as large a volume of buildings, and coal was higher in price.

In the summer of 1915 I wrote again to Mr. Pratt, and tried to point out the problem in all its aspects. I urged a change in personnel, and a more businesslike administration. I could have made no greater mistake. After all, was it any of my business! Had not the trustees taken such matters completely out of my hands, and assumed full responsibility for the operation of the college?

In vain I argued that a good college must be good all through, that students discontented about their meals were not good students, and that teachers dissatisfied with the ways of their life would not give their best to the college. I should have known that my protests would be quite naturally interpreted as a desire to secure more power for myself. Perhaps they were. Who knows? One could not stand by as a mere onlooker without wanting to make the college more efficient. Certainly I had become greatly interested in kitchen and boiler house, pumps and dynamos, sewers and coal supply, farm and garden, watchmen and groundsmen, and all the intricacies through which our money passed. People asked me about them, and I did not like to confess my ignorance or my lack of authority.

I should have remembered, for I soon observed it, that the New York trustees looked upon Vassar as their playground. To visit it and its gardens was their holiday. They did not come to consider its problems closely, though they doubtless enjoyed their brief authority during the short periods of meeting. Women's education was their romance, taking them back to youth and beauty.

"Dear lady," said Mr. Pratt; and the other trustees, every time they spoke to an alumna trustee, a woman professor, or indeed any other member of the fair sex, never used any other formula. "Dear ladies!"

"Dear college!" was their thought. Often ruthless and quite arbitrary in action, they were utterly sentimental about Vassar life. It was a fountain sealed, a walled garden. Their lives did not have much aesthetic outlet, and the pretty college took it all. They wanted pretty stories from me, not rude realities. I was nonplussed. Yet they were very generous and helpful, in their fashion. They loved to dream about its problems, but not to act on them. Occasionally, their dreams would take form in the gift of a building or a professorship. Mr. Dimock often brought a rare book for the library. Dr. Sanders brought five most beautiful etchings of Rembrandt and Haden. "Costly offerings, rich and rare," were Alma Mater's due. Every one of them had some sentimental cousinship to Vassar. It was a beautiful and even tender relation. Why disturb it with any practical reform?

For the overall totals the trustees could not be censored. The college was solvent. Its income exceeded its expenses by over fifty thousand a year. The change from gas to electricity had been efficiently carried out, the expense charged to this surplus over a period of years. A new dial phone system was being installed, limited to the campus. The dial was, however, ahead of its time, and was out of order all too often. But the college funds had been well protected, and a good rise of interest was paid on a capital equal to every dollar the college had received for endowment. Something over a hundred thousand of endowment for scholarships was invested in Jewett Hall; this was regarded as reasonable at the time. When it was possible, I asked that this be repaid and the sum reinvested in securities, which was done.

Everything depended on discretion, the discretion of the trustees and the discretion of its officers. There was no check whatever upon expenditures otherwise, except that the accounts were audited annually. The proper supervision by the Executive Committee had been fairly adequate in the days of the smaller college, but the local committee stood in the way of business checkup, and the committee was mostly concerned with petty detail. At every meeting Mr. Pelton objected to every expenditure, and grudgingly yielded only when the vote contained the proviso "that it be done without expense to the college." This phrase became proverbial at our meetings.

There was a third group of trustees to whom none of these observations applied—the women members. Among them Florence M. Cushing, already mentioned, was predominant. A member of the distinguished Boston family and a householder in old

Walnut Street on Boston Hill, Miss Cushing was both of the old and the new. Her house was unheated, save by an occasional grate fire. I have never been so cold anywhere as when a guest of Miss Cushing's. She was the self-approved guardian of Boston Common and the Public Garden, and the city owed much to her. Boston alumnae were the strongest group in the association. When she was younger, Miss Cushing had led them in an attack on President Caldwell, and after a rather bitter fight, had driven him from his position. Thereafter, these alumnae had sat on the Board, "by invitation." Maria Mitchell had urged Miss Cushing as the proper President to succeed Caldwell, but Taylor had been chosen. They were not yet ready to try a woman.

Miss Cushing had served the college for a short time in the seventies as librarian, and she understood its operation better than any of her men associates. She had insisted on improvement of the college as a household, and as chairman of a committee on Amenities had succeeded in some improvements. Her battles with Mr. Pelton were memorable. Jewett Hall was her bête noire, and she never forgave Mr. Pelton for his share in the ugly edifice. He on his part thought it a fine building, and the fight *de gustibus* became very gusty indeed.

But the women of the Board were better businessmen than the men. They were not permitted on any committee that concerned itself with essential business, nor had they authority over any branch of college affairs. Nevertheless they made their voices heard.

When war came to the United States and to the college, in the beginning of my third year in office, the "local committee" was working on the problem of a new heating plant. Whether it was really needed or not no one knew, but Mr. Adriance said it was, and his committee got authority to proceed. Costs steadily mounted, and finally only second-hand boilers could be obtained, because of the government's need of metal. Before its completion in 1918 the project amounted to some two hundred thousand dollars. In the meantime college costs had risen in all other departments, leaving no surplus for payment of the new plant. Mr. Adriance, frightened, looked around for a scapegoat; and of course the President was ready at hand. I had not been consulted, nor had I been on the committee, but after all, I ought to have known somehow all that might happen and be prepared for it.

It was easy to shift the blame on my shoulders, and in a sense I was to blame for not knowing enough to make perfectly clear to all the trustees just how the college was run. But I was a young man, and was much troubled not to be in the war in a more active capacity. Governor Whitman had made me Chief of the Division of Instruction in the State Council of Defense, and the trustees had released me on half time to carry on this work. Later, in September, 1917, I was appointed National Director of the Junior Membership of the American Red Cross, and had also taken responsibility for organizing the first great Red Cross membership campaign in December. Twenty-two million dollars came in, in dollar memberships. For this service I had been released from two-thirds of my college time. Both positions were at my own cost, and I lived on one-third of my regular salary, without compensation from the State or the American Red Cross.

Here was a good ground for the assumption that I had lost my interest in the college, and had taken on other tasks from which I should be completely released. The other trustees from Poughkeepsie agreed with Mr. Adriance on this point. The next step was to sound out the Executive Committee.

Mr. Pratt was the key to this group. He had great business worries and his son was overseas at the front. Moreover, he was far from well. Premonitions of the illness which overtook him two years later were already evident in loss of memory and in other ways. He was appalled at the situation and took immediate steps. The Executive Committee, at its September meeting, granted me leave of absence for the year, with the understanding that I should resign at the end of the year.

Then came the victory for the women. I had been ill, and

went to Old Point Comfort to recuperate from my influenza.
The women trustees led by Mrs. Arthur H. Hadley and Mrs.
John Wood Blodgett appealed to the full Board, and though
the Executive Committee was sustained, the majority was slim.
The faculty, the alumnae, and the students investigated in turn,
and demanded that the trustees rescind their action.

Miss Cushing alone among the women kept with the Committee but called on Marjorie to confess her regret. "I want you
to know, Mrs. MacCracken," she said, "that whatever we may
think of your husband, there is only one opinion about you."

Still Marjorie was not pleased.

To test the student reaction, a group of trustees came to the
college and went to evening chapel. They were sent to Coventry
by the whole body of students, who stared them down until they
were terrified.

The president of the senior class, it was said, wrote to her
uncle, a trustee: "Drop the hat when you are ready, Uncle
George, you'll be in it up to your neck."

The students carried the day. The war was ending, and
people were more cheerful. The deficit did not seem so important. The trustees held a special meeting, on November 11, 1918,
of all days, and unanimously requested my immediate return to
the college. I agreed to this, insisting rather foolishly that they
hear my side of the case. This they did in good part, and I returned to the college, in the midst of rejoicing over peace. The
faculty literally danced through the rooms of the President's
House that night, while the students rioted outside.

Next morning the Executive Committee met with me as if
nothing had happened. A few weeks later, Mr. H. P. Davison of
the American Red Cross wrote Mr. Pratt to ask him to release
me, in order that I might go to the Versailles Conference to
assist him in the organization of the International League of Red
Cross Societies. Mr. Pratt refused. My presence, he said, was
indispensable at the college.

I told the trustees I would assume full responsibility for the deficit. Mr. Pratt thereupon most generously offered to match dollar for dollar whatever was given. We raised in six weeks over two hundred thousand dollars, and the year ended without a deficit and with a respectable reserve. Meantime I set myself to regain the confidence of my critics on the Board, and by the end of the year had the good fortune to welcome each of them at my home. The sequel came two years later, when the University of Buffalo asked me to be its chancellor, offering a much larger salary. The Vassar trustees urged me to stay, and voted to reorganize the Board and the college on my terms. I accepted on this basis, without accepting a salary increase. The reorganization took three years, and was a joint enterprise by alumnae, faculty, and trustees. From that time date the printed Bylaws, the Academic Statute, the Declaration of Relations between Trustees and Faculty, including the guaranty of academic freedom and the principle of conference on all vital questions; the fully organized and implemented system of budgeting, the chart of business organization with its orders in clarification, the welfare and pension funds of the employees and faculty; provision for conference, the recognition of the students' share in the college government; in a word, a modern college came to fruition, some seeds of which were sown during the days of my apprenticeship.

GOLDEN DAYS

MY STORY HAS NOT been a personal one, I see, as I glance back over these pages. Even Marjorie, who is much too lenient a critic, suggested that it might be confusing to readers if, at my first mention of her, I did not include our marital state. I remedied that lack, but I'm afraid I'm just as impersonal as ever. It is a fault inherent in the temperament, that I have preferred many good friends rather than one all-absorbing friendship, held by "hoops of steel."

Though believing in the primary values of personality, I sought instinctively the approach through environment, action, and ideas, rather than by emotion. From feelings I shied away at once. I remember one day at an interview, when Miss Wylie said to me: "Mr. President, on this matter I feel—" I interrupted her: "Tell me what you think, not what you feel." She was disconcerted, but in a moment collected herself and said: "I think you are right. We are too emotional at Vassar."

Whether it was the intense friction generated by the underlying forces at Vassar by the close and isolated life of a country college, or by the new situation of authority in the life of women, I never knew, but certainly life at Vassar was always tense in the year 1915. There was a something in the air, vital, eager, excited, that infected the spirit. It was *not* just youth. The oldest teacher felt it. It was a feeling compounded of all the things I have said, and many more, I am sure. And oddly, I could not express my own sense of it, then or later.

"You don't need to be so shy with us," said a student one day.

"Loosen up." I tried to follow her advice, but it was no use. They had to take me as I was, someone who would play, work, think, with all good will, but who never gave any friend a key to his city of the spirit, or closed its outer wards to the newcomer.

One of the foreign students rushed over to pour out the woes of her Slavic heart upon my wife's kind breast. "Nobody *lofes* me," she sobbed. "I must go home." "Why my dear," said Marjorie, "you are mistaken. Everyone likes you here at Vassar. I don't know anyone they like more." "Oh yes, they like me, I know; but nobody *lofes* me," with a fresh burst of tears.

I was like that. I could never achieve the adoration of other college leaders, or be the confidant of all my colleagues. Still more, I could not build a party among the faculty, though a clear policy inevitably creates a majority and minority group. But these were always fluid. My suggestions never produced the same vote in any two meetings. I decided in my first year that the English system would be mine, and that any adverse action on an important proposal would involve my immediate resignation. There was none. A vigorous faculty group was already there, ready to move, and all they wanted was leadership and not much of that. I felt like Teddy Roosevelt at San Juan Hill, who replied to an admirer gushing about his Rough Rider dash: "Nothing brave about it. I had to run, you know. I would have been stepped on."

When ten years had passed, and a strong group of colleagues of my own age had developed, comrades in many a tussle on the floor of debate, we would once in a while get together calling ourselves "the roaring Forties," and laughing at our impetuous attacks on the established order. We were all good friends together.

One after another, the older professors had sought to take over the direction of my mind, for the good of the college. My shyness proved my best protection. There was nothing to hold onto, in my rather slippery temper. Miss Salmon came closest perhaps to success with me, but she loved too much a fight for its own sake. She came in my office one day after a victory. "Now let's tear things wide open." I wasn't made that way.

We never tried to know very many students. We let it be known that we were "at home" on Thursdays every week. Those might come who wished. Many did, many did not. I never tried consciously to remember names, in this being far inferior to Marjorie. I could meet an alumna three times in a month, and still have to get a jog in the memory. It was always a handicap.

Yet of contacts as between person and person there were plenty. "What do you think you're doing?" said a trustee to me, as I arose from third base after being called "out" on my slide for it which had resulted in my colliding violently with a student third baseman. "I am just following your advice, sir," I said. "You urged me to come in contact with the student body. I have just come in contact, and hard." When in 1946 the faculty honored me with a "party," "Life Begins at Sixty-five," John Peirce *in mea persona* sang "I Love the Student Body."

Our friendships were almost always of the classroom, the tennis court, the picnic at John Burroughs', or of some conference, some problem of conduct, some new project. I could not, and did not, urge my views in chapel exercises. Rather, I came to know well the leaders of student life, through them my plans filtered out to the whole group, not by any force other than mere gravitation.

Marjorie always urged me especially in crises, to talk more often and more urgently. "They want to know what you think. Tell them." I did it very rarely and only under strong pressure of events.

"What an opportunity you have here, MacCracken, presiding over these eleven hundred young women, to mould character and lay deep foundations of principle." I acknowledged the opportunity, but could not use it, for it was not in me. I was all dressed up, and nowhere to go, because I just was not built to enjoy in any form the exercise of authority.

As I look back after thirty years, thinking of Matthew Vassar's dream of a college where ladies might learn to become intelligently useful, then of Dr. Taylor's conservatism—"One thing has not changed and will never change—the need of a soul for its own development, for resource, for mental breadth, and outlook, unharried by immediate needs, or the fancied call of a sphere that may never be aught but a fancy or a vision"—it seems to me that my temperament, though it held me back from powerful leadership, was not ill suited to working in a general movement toward education *in* life. For fifty years students went to Vassar and hung their clothes on the hickory limb, but didn't go near the water. They were told that they must be better women before they could make life better. Dr. Taylor, in his fiery defense of the early Vassar, which leads off the volume of Fiftieth Anniversary addresses, cried to his audience: "Where shall we put our chief emphasis? That is the question. On bread, or on 'every word of God'?"

Along with this fundamental position went a most careful supervision of personal manners and conduct. Our wardens took the greatest pains in persuading the young women not to use lipstick. An atmosphere of the boarding-school pervaded the residence and rules were relaxed long after social convention had sanctioned the change in city life.

But by 1915 we were ready to go swimming, leaving our clothes on the old hickory limb, and finding in the adventure either confirmation by the test of experience of the validity of old authority, or the way to a more self-reliant view of life.

The comparison of a catalogue of 1915 with that of 1945 will help to make this clear. There was one semester of American literature offered in 1915, today there are five, with other courses in contemporary novel, press, and poetry. The Department of Bible has become a department of comparative religion, with separate courses in religions of India, of China, and of Japan. In art, music, and drama, against a few theoretical lectures, a fully articulated structure with recognition of "performance." Anthropology, sociology, child study, and human geography are completely new departments, as is Russian. In the sciences, to take zoology as example, new aspects are heredity, experimental embryology and ecology. Everywhere there are both expansion of field and greater thoroughness of method.

Yet nothing has been dropped. That is the remarkable fact, and it points to the basis of my own stand. There is no contradiction between "pure" and "applied," between theory and performance, between thought and action. Some actions are thoughtless, no doubt, but many are not. In reality, and it has always been so, thought and action are one and the same thing.

At the bottom of the attack on practical studies is an aristocratic distaste for labor, for menial and manual routine. By denying the possibility of any intellectual concern with "bread," for example, Dr. Taylor set it outside of "every word of God." Yet a science of nutrition, new since his day, has done more to improve the world's health than any other step.

Vassar in 1915 broke with this dualism of mind and matter. Both are energy. The college embraced the view of the Founder, that education should be more practical. The *Past with reference to the Present,* the *Theory with reference to Performance, Thinking with reference to action,* these were its major principles. I said in my inaugural address, "This is, then, what college has to offer the student—the genius of modern life. . . ." "And whatever of special stimulus its students are to have will come from their sense of unity with its main purpose, the cause of learning."

In this interpretation, the genius (the prevailing temper or spirit, as the dictionary defines it) of modern life will determine the *thing* studied, while the *process* of learning will bring the interest, the sustaining purpose. On this theory Vassar went forth to meet its second half-century.

Through these pages there has run, as a sort of connecting thread, this idea of a half century completed. The Fiftieth Anniversary, the first widely heralded occasion of the kind, took place October 10–13, 1915. Vassar seized its golden opportunity. "The celebration was an expression of the will and energy of a united community." Constance M. Rourke, the "chronicler" who wrote this, was later the famous critic of American literature. She knew whereof she wrote, and was not writing mere publicity, for she was a teacher at Vassar. Amy Reed, the general chairman, had forty committees working under her of faculty, alumnae, and students, while trustee committees stood by and furnished ample funds for a new outdoor theater, new walks, for publication, concerts, and all the minor costs. It was indeed, in its lavishness, Medicean. To quote Constance Rourke again, "If the success of the experiment involved in the founding of the college were in need of proof, surely that proof would exist in the ease and confidence, the pleasure and zest, with which the college of today, now grown to a full sense of power, united for creative effort, producing a celebration which was not only memorable in idea and purpose, but touched with beauty."

Her book, and my memory, bear out the claim.

A dozen major addresses marked four days of morning sessions. Alumnae business occupied the afternoons, for during the celebrations a hundred thousand dollars brought the Anniversary Fund up to a third of its promised million. Exhibits of art and evenings of music by Noble on the organ and two concerts by the Russian Symphony were highlights. Meanwhile steadily through the celebration the students held an intercollegiate conference on the function of non-academic activities in college life. Most of the eastern colleges, and some western sent delegates. Bryn Mawr alone declined, as Miss Thomas did not approve. Yet the report as it stands shows how serious and how concerned the delegates were. Their criticism was searching, but much was brought out that showed a correlation of academic study with non-academic activity, and an increasing effort to bring the great issues of the World War and national life upon the campus.

Of all the activities for which I have no room here, one stands out in memory, "The Pageant of Athena." It was, of course, the heyday of pageantry, and the students had not only many good models, but a good director in Hazel Mackaye. Working for two years on their script, the students produced a cooperative story of women's intellectual advancement, in a charming way. Edna St. Vincent Millay as Marie de France, in a recital of her *lais*, was perhaps the loveliest of all the many scenes. Eleanor Goss, later a noted tennis player, was superb as Hortensia.

At the close of the performance my wife's brother, Lee W. Dodd, himself a critic, poet, and playwright, rushed off to my study and buried himself for an hour. The result was a poem, printed here for the first time.

I saw the same glow of feeling a few days ago, when a Polish alumna of 1932 walked with me about the campus. For eleven years she had been a displaced person, and her story was tragic. You would think she could have no further use for tears. Yet as we stood in the Shakespeare Garden, they were shining in her eyes.

THE PAGEANT OF ATHENA

Vassar; October, 1915

These gracious women and noble, summoned forth
From the pale past for symbols—let them fade . . .
But ye who summon, who draw, who guide them hither
With your grave maiden thought and delicate
Alluring gestures to this sacred grove,
Fade not—forsake me not! We need the sight,
The sound, the unwearying hope, the youth of you
Here on this brain-sick, bitter Earth, half-crazed
In a crimson frenzy . . .
                                        Ah fade not! Stay! I feel
Even in the Courts of Autumn—feel on my cheek
A breath as it were of April . . . nor all the rust
And ruin of lifeless leaves shall blur my dream
Of reawakening beauty—young grass and gold
Imponderable of the spring's first daffodils.

LEE WILSON DODD